Knight Shift

Knight Shift

Written by: Suzanne LaVoie

Published by: Heather Andrews

Follow It Thru Publishing

Edited by: Julie Kapuschak

Graphics by: Lorraine Shulba

Published by:

Heather Andrews http://publishing.followitthru.com/, www.followitthru.com

Book and cover design by Lorraine Shulba: www.bluebugstudios.com

Editing and Manuscript compilation by Julie Kapuschak: www.juliemaye.com

Formatting by Bojan Kratofil: https://www.facebook.com/bojan.kratofil

ISBN: 978-1- 5136-2928-5

"To live a life fulfilled reflects on the things you have with gratitude."

—Jaren Davis

There are no words sufficient enough to properly express the amount of gratitude I feel for all of the individuals in my life whom have been and continue to be a colossal part of my journey. While I could devote an entire chapter to listing all of the names responsible for helping lead me to where I am today, I will attempt to consolidate what I am able to on this page.

First and foremost, I am super thankful for my mother Marlyn LaVoie, who has been my rock, my biggest cheerleader, my inspiration, and the one person who has always believed in me and my dreams and goals, especially to be a full-time writer.

I want to express immense gratitude to some of the most amazing friends a woman could ever ask for, especially Jennifer C., Reverend Elizabeth E., Janet and Steve H., Chris and Karen S., Peter and Sue H., Ginny P., Pastor Tracie P., John P., and Florence M. You all mean the world to me and always will!

I notably want to thank Cheryl Raley from the Charlroy Motel (Owner), Seaside Park and Annette Dorman, whom were both the catalysts and mentors (and friends) for me engaging in a new career path with hospitality and tourism for thirteen years and are still so important to me. I am especially grateful for Cheryl believing in my ability to learn new skills within the industry and my personal life.

This book would not have come about if it hadn't been for my absolutely amazing literary team, including my incredible and supportive publisher Heather Andrews, my highly creative and energetic graphic designer Lorraine Shulba, and multi-talented and encouraging editor Julie Kapuschak. I also want to thank Author Kristie Knights, who allowed me the opportunity to be part of a book compilation over a year ago and has remained a wonderful friend.

Last but not least, I am grateful for the gorgeous and alluring Adirondack region, especially the village of Lake George and all of the lovely people I have had the privilege to meet over decades of traveling there (specifically the Marinelli family, Christy R., and Dan R.). This book is a tribute to all that I love about the area and pray others will come to love it too. There are so many others that I would love to acknowledge here, but know that you are given thanks for in my heart.

Table of Contents

Foreword

An ounce of courage and a leap of faith…

We each desire to belong, to be loved just as we are. Often in life there are circumstances when we are left out, discarded, alone, and yearning for a sense of acceptance and purpose.

Dreams have been destroyed, and forgotten. We have each experienced great loss that caused our world to ignite, come aflame, and destroy our heart and soul; only to smolder till we can inhale and reach for courage.

In the depth of the darkness it feels as if there is no way out. However, what we often forget is it takes twenty seconds of courage to change a life. If we are lucky, the twenty seconds of courage leads to a ripple of inspiration and change for the positive for those around us as well.

Meet Sage Knight; in the wake of destruction as she is smoldering; she has a choice just like you. She can reach for more darkness and self-pity, or she can grapple with the light and embrace the journey. Step in the shoes of Sage as she recounts tough times, yet inspires a town in despair. She had no idea her twenty seconds of courage would lead a town to a place of prosperity and purpose. Of course, what you see on the outside is not often the case in the inside. Nothing is more-true of the journey of Sage Knight and the town she resides.

Join Sage on a journey of self-discovery, digging deep to trust thyself, and the rebuilding of a life; not only her own, but those around her as well. You will fall in love with Sage Knight as she embraces the new life she is creating while giving back to those around her as they are inspired to achieve the dreams they have let go of so long ago.

The Knight Shift will envelop you in a sea of inspiration from a place of brokenness, to the triumph of a life created to give purpose to others. Bask in the sun of Sage Knight as she shares a story lived by you and I. Find comfort in the power of pain which leads to a life of joy. Come along and make the shift, the Knight Shift, to a place of grace, peace, and empowerment!

Kristie Knights, LPC

Psychotherapist and Mediator

www.kristieknights.com

Chapter 1

The clock in my bedroom was flashing 10:03 AM. I have been getting spoiled with being able to sleep late most mornings, but I know this can't last forever. The soft sound of the breeze coming off of the lake from a block away filled my room. It was a welcomed and familiar sound.

My name is Sage Knight, I am single, and my age is still in the accepted bracket of being considered a younger adult. Chronologically, I know what the number is, but at this stage of the game, I seriously question the reality of it. Knight is not my maiden name, but it encourages me on those days when I could use a boost of energy to face the day. I picture myself as one of those medieval tin men statues I have seen at yard sales with every arrow coming my way just bouncing off of me into oblivion. Or, I am gleefully reminded of one of my favorite shows growing up, Knight Rider, and find myself wishing some days I could ride off into the sunset with the main actor and the computerized talking car. Hey, one can still dream, right?

I made myself a cup of tea and sat in my favorite rocking lounge chair. My studio apartment is small, but it's mine and it allows me to feel I still have some sense of control in my life. The apartment is also manageable for me, as I prefer a place that isn't high maintenance. I have been blessed with a wonderful landlord, Paul, who has also become a good friend. He saw me through some tough transitions and always responds right away if a problem occurs in the apartment. I try not to bother Paul unless it is an absolute mess of a task that I cannot take care of myself. Of course, if it is electrical, plumbing that requires more than a bucket solution, a non-functioning AC or heater…well, hopefully, these would all happen at different times so he does not put up the sign of the cross when I call. So far, it has been a month since I have needed anything fixed, so I believe I am safe. To put it in a nutshell, I am basically starting over. Certain decks of cards were handed to me that I was not expecting, and my life was filled with heart-breaking emotional earthquakes. I used to joke with my close friends that I should have "fault coverage" due to all of the tremors and aftershocks. I was not expecting to be single again, but this is my present reality, and I am moving forward one tiny step at a time.

After two cups of tea and listening to the windy conversation of ripples breaking on the lake beach, I decided to join the land of the living and take a stroll to the nearby walkway. It was February, but it was quiet and peaceful at this time of year. I have no other neighbors at this time, but I admit I have been keeping to myself over the past couple of months, anyway. I visit with my parents who live in proximity of my town, and I have gone out with a few select friends, but that has been the extent of my social life. I also lost a recent job position due to a serious illness I had, and I was told the spot could not be held open any longer. *How compassionate,* I thought. *NOT!* Now, I am questioning what will come next.

I put on my overused, favorite red leather jacket and took the short walk to the little beach. A couple of other water-seeking souls were out there as well, including a man exploring the sand with a metal detector. "Good luck", I whispered in the soft wind to him. Even though it was still winter, the weather was not filled with a biting chill. I don't do well with extreme cold or heat spells. I prefer the fall, although I love living in a state where there are four seasons.

I heard some noise and looked toward the direction of the man with the metal detector. Apparently, he found something and appeared very pleased with his discovery. *Seek and you shall find,* as quoted by Jesus Christ in the Bible. I wish they came out with a metal detector for life situations, although I believe that is what prayer is. I sat on one of the benches and stared at the beckoning lake. I don't know why, but at that moment the tears just spilled out of my eyes. If anyone came by and noticed, I could blame it on the cold. But, in that moment, I realized that the man with the metal detector was a message for me. I needed to seek and find what my next step was. I looked up toward the bluish-gray sky and asked for something, anything, to help me get out of this stagnant pool in my mind and heart.

Chapter 2

I checked my watch and saw that I had been sitting on the bench for nearly an hour. This did the mind and body well. I felt more focused and a bit lighter than before I left the apartment. I was so entranced by the lake and what was happening within me emotionally that I didn't observe the others leave, including metal detector man. At that moment, I was starting to feel chilled, so I headed back to my place. Before I left the lake, I took in the surroundings of motels, houses, and other buildings. In a couple of months, seasonal businesses would soon be opening, and the crowds would return for summer fun and enjoyment. Being in the mountains meant there were also winter activities, but not as much as the months between May and September. One huge perk of where I was living was that I did not have to worry about parking here; I had my own spot in the driveway. Growing up, the local amusement park was one of my most cherished places to hang out at. To this day, I still go on rides and I don't care who is watching.

On my way back to the apartment, I took notice of a sign posted on one of the motel's side glass doors advertising for help at the front desk. It was called the Serenity Savor Motel. I liked the name, the façade, and the outdoor pool. It had that old motel charm to it. As I stood there on the sidewalk, I seriously considered inquiring. I have always enjoyed the hotel atmosphere whenever I traveled, and I needed a job. Heck, I needed a fresh start. What did I have to lose? I have worked with people in many different settings, so it wouldn't be too hard.

I walked back fast to my apartment and called the number of the motel. The call was answered immediately.

"Hello, Serenity Savor Motel. May I help you?" a female voice asked.

"Hello, my name is Sage Knight, and I actually just live down the road. I was passing by your motel on the way back from the lake and saw your sign advertising for help. Are you still looking for someone?"

"Yes, I am. Do you have hospitality experience?"

"No," I started, already anticipating a rejection, "but I do have a lot of experience in jobs that revolve around serving the public."

"That's fine. When are you available to come in and meet?"

"I am available this afternoon and tomorrow."

"How about tomorrow morning at eleven? I have somewhere to go later today."

"Eleven works for me. May I ask your name?"

She answered, "Renee. Renee Randoll."

"Great! I look forward to meeting with you tomorrow at eleven, Renee."

"Same here."

After the conversation ended, I sat down in my rocker and questioned whether this was the right move for me. It was totally different from what I had done for work before, or what I had studied in school. Again, what did I have to lose? After all, this was a much needed interview, and Renee sounded very nice on the phone. Tomorrow would be a new step. To celebrate, I drove to a local restaurant, treated myself to dinner, and immersed myself into my latest book. I am very comfortable going to places by myself, which isn't always the case with some people I know. It works for me, especially when I am invested in a novel where I just have to find out what happens next.

I called my parents that night and informed them of my interview the next day. They both wished me luck and understood that I needed a change ever since the recent heart-breaking events in my life. I managed to find one of my resume copies and picked out a professional-looking outfit. I love the pinstripe look but that seemed a bit too formal, especially for this area. I didn't want to show up too casual, either. I finally settled on a nice pair of dress pants and a sharp top. I also selected what jewelry I was going to wear: one of my cross necklaces and a pair of gold hoop earrings. I felt pleased with what I chose and hoped Renee would approve. I went to bed that night with more hope than I have felt for a long, long time.

Chapter 3

I woke up the next morning way before my alarm went off. I laid there anticipating what kind of questions I would be asked at my interview. Truthfully, I was still bummed from having to resign from my teaching job. Being in the hospital for a serious gastrointestinal infection and weeks of recovery slammed the hammer on that. I don't always understand why there isn't more compassion in the workplace. I certainly did not ask to be sick. Now there is nothing I can do about it except move forward, whatever that meant for me now.

I drank my usual cup of tea and ate breakfast while reading my book. When it got to be around ten, I showered and took my time dressing for my appointment. I wanted to make sure I looked my best. I applied makeup to hide the stress marks that may have been more imaginary than real. Then, I put my resume in a manila folder left over from my teaching supplies and headed over to the Serenity Savor Motel. I felt a lot of nerves in my stomach, but I pressed on. I walked up the steps to the main lobby and saw the sign on the front desk requesting the person to pick up the phone and let it ring if no one was there. I looked around and since there was no one in sight, I followed the instructions on the sign. Sure enough, I heard the phone ringing. After a few seconds, a door by the desk opened and a woman came out to the lobby.

"Well, you passed the first test." she said.

The woman must have seen the confused look on my face because she pointed to the phone.

"You actually followed the directions on the sign. That's a plus. If you do wind up working here, you will see that's not always the case."

"You must be Renee Randoll."

"Yes. And I'm sorry—your name again?"

"Sage Knight. It's a pleasure to meet you."

"Likewise. So you live down the road? Well, that would be very convenient for you if you take the job."

To be honest, I hadn't considered that, but Renee was right. No commuting issues for me!

"Please come in and we can talk. My husband and I live on the property in the adjoining house along with my daughter."

I followed Renee into her house, which was a nice size. She pointed to one of the couches and I sat down, following her lead. Renee offered me coffee, which I was very grateful for. For some reason when I am nervous coffee seems to relax me.

"So…what made you decide to apply to this position? I know you said you never worked in hospitality before."

Now, here's the thing, how much should I divulge? Should I mention that this was a fresh start? That my life changed in ways that I never imagined? Please have mercy on me? I decided to just go with the flow at that point.

"To be honest, I am looking for something new. I had to leave my last job, which was a teaching job, because I was ill for a few weeks. I am fine now in case you're wondering. I love the lake and thought it would be fun to work by it."

The game show Jeopardy theme started playing in my head as I saw Renee considering what I just said. I handed her the folder with my resume.

"Here's my resume if you wanted to take a look."

Renee accepted it and looked it over. Time always seems to slow down when you are waiting for someone to make a decision, doesn't it?

"Wow, you do have a lot of experience in other areas. You have your Bachelor's Degree? Very impressive."

"Thank you." It was all I could manage to say at that moment.

"You don't plan to go back to teaching?"

I decided to just let it all out. What did I have to lose?

"I have been going through a lot of changes in my life. Ones that I didn't see coming. I guess that's life, right? Being told to leave my last job did a number on me, especially because I was sick. I need something new; something fun. So, here I am."

I said the last part with a big smile and spread my arms out. Nothing like adding a little drama to the mix. Truthfully, I figured I was toast at this point anyway. I thought my career in hospitality was over before it even began. To my surprise, though, Renee announced, "Well, I haven't received any other calls, and I appreciate your honesty. I also am impressed by your resume. I believe this could work out. How about you come back in two weeks to start training? I usually open mid-April, and I would like to have you ready to go by then."

I was so stunned I didn't reply right away. So, Renee asked, "Is that okay with you?"

"Uh…yes. Yes! Sorry, I wasn't sure how this was going to go."

"I understand; a lot more than you know. Someday we'll talk about it. In the meantime, I will plan for you to begin training on February 23rd. Come back here around eleven that day."

"I will be here! Thank you so much!"

We stood up and shook hands.

"Thank you. Now I can take that sign down, finally."

I left there feeling so excited that I literally felt like skipping down the block back to my apartment. I really liked Renee, and I felt this would be a great starting over point for me. I could not wait until February 23rd, where a new journey was about to begin.

Chapter 4

The next two weeks seemed to fly by. I had already informed my parents and friends about what I would be doing. I felt like my parents were a little disappointed that I wasn't going back to teaching because they felt that it was my biggest gift. Ultimately, they understood that I needed time to deal with everything that happened, and funds were dwindling. I didn't want to let them down, but I felt that I should at least give the motel a chance. *Who knows? I may even like it more than teaching!* I thought.

On the morning of February 23rd I got up early, but I had a stomach full of nerves again. Ever since the changes, my self-doubt crept up on me like mold on food that had been left out too long. I am not the poster child for self-confidence, even though I achieved successful grades during high school and college. I was even part of honor societies and had received a couple of significant scholarships. My grades were the only thing I felt like I didn't have to play catch-up with. Now, it was time to move on to a new path.

Renee had informed me earlier in the week that I could come to work in jeans and a sweatshirt because I was training and the motel was not open yet. I welcomed this, as casual clothing would help ease some of the nerves. It sounds silly, but for me, dressing down allows me to relax more and take in what is being said to me. I feel like the majority of my brain cells have been fried like eggs, and the remaining ones are hanging on for dear life.

I got myself together and headed over to Serenity Savor. Yes, Lord, I could use a lot of serenity at this point! The side lobby door was open so I walked in. I was thankful I wore a heavy sweatshirt under my leather jacket because it was cold in there. *The place was not open for business yet, so what is the sense in running the heat in the lobby?* I thought. I just had to deal with it, even if I wound up the color of a Smurf at the end of the day.

Renee must have heard me and read my thoughts because she stepped out of her house immediately.

"Why don't you come inside? I am just finishing up with making coffee. Plus, it's freezing out here anyway."

I followed her inside and sat on the same couch I did over two weeks ago. This time a brown cat was in the living room. He or she sat in front of me and stared directly at me; probably wondering if I am friend or foe.

"Cute cat!" I called out.

"Oh, that's Mocha. Is she staring at you yet?"

"Oh, yes." I said.

"She does that with anyone new in here. The last time you were here she stayed in my bedroom. If you come back a second time, then she checks you out. If you are here a while, eventually she will jump on your lap. I hope you like cats."

"Yes. I love all animals actually."

"That's another plus. I don't have patience for people who don't like animals. They treat you better than most humans at times."

I admit, I had to agree. Renee brought out two mugs of coffee. Mocha stood her position with me, even with Renee being in the room. I started feeling a little warm in the house, so I removed my jacket and laid it beside me. No sooner did I put it down, Mocha jumped on top of it and sprawled out all over.

"So that's what you were after, huh?" I asked Mocha, shaking my head.

"It was probably the red. She seems to like bold colors. I hope you don't mind."

"Nah. I think it's funny."

Renee began talking to me about how she loved the motel business and the area itself. I got to meet her daughter, Heather, that morning as well. I still hadn't met her husband, but he worked as a ski instructor in the winter during the day. By the afternoon, I was feeling pretty relaxed. Mocha even left the comfort of my jacket and graduated to my lap. It made me think about the two parakeets I owned a couple of years back. I thought about owning birds again, but I felt like I had to get other situations in my life back on track before bringing pets into the mix.

Renee spent part of the afternoon showing me around the motel. Tomorrow, she would begin training me on the computer program she uses for the business. There was a lot to learn, which was why she wanted me to get started right away. She also informed me that I would primarily work weekends until it got closer to the end of May. Then, gradually, I would take on more days, and then I would have a full-time schedule for the ten-week summer season.

"At this point, I need you for the night shift which is 3 to 11. Heather works 7 to 3."

"I am fine with that. No problem."

"Good. You should chat with her. She can fill you in on some of the interesting stories that have happened here and be an extra trainer as well."

"I will definitely do that."

Renee had decided that we would just start fresh with the computer tomorrow and call it a day. By now I was feeling a lot better about working here than I did this morning. I thanked her for everything and headed home.

Chapter 5

As I was approaching my apartment, I saw a familiar dark blue truck in the driveway. A door opened from the main entryway, and Paul stepped out with a tool box in hand.

"Knight, hi!"

Paul has always called me Knight.

"Hey, Paul! What are you doing here? It must feel strange responding to a problem here that isn't from me."

He chuckled and said, "Yes, it does feel strange. Just kidding. You may have a new neighbor in a few weeks. I am checking on what needs to be updated in that particular unit. Seriously, though, how are you?"

"Well, I got a new job."

"Awesome! Where?"

"Believe it or not, the Serenity Savor Motel just up the block."

"Well, I am happy for you. I really am. To be honest, I was worried about you. I know you went through a huge loss, but it seemed…like you were giving up on life."

"Wow, landlord by day, psychologist by night."

I realized I sounded a bit curt when I said that, so I quickly apologized.

"Sorry, that was really rude of me. You have been nothing but nice and supportive. See, this is why I haven't been hanging out with too many people. I am still very bitter about everything."

Paul put the toolbox down in the back of his truck and leaned up against the tailgate.

"Look, I get it. You have every right to be bitter. Unfortunately, I have seen crap like this happen to a lot of good people. I don't begin to understand it. All I know is, and you may not see it right now, your life isn't over. Jeez, Knight, you're only in your thirties! Even if you were in your fifties or sixties, there is still life!"

Paul opened his toolbox and took out a hammer.

"Are you going to knock some sense into me?" I joked.

"One thing you have not lost is your sense of humor. Seriously, listen to me. This hammer can be looked at in two ways. It can be used to knock down something, used to demolish, which is what happened to you. This same hammer is also used to rebuild. That's what I was just doing before you came back home. You need to rebuild, which is what you are doing by taking that job. It's like most anything that we deal with in life. You can let it destroy you or use it to build something else."

I shook my head.

"Paul, you are a wonderful landlord, but you certainly missed your calling as a therapist."

"My mother was a school psychologist. I am used to a lot of different perspectives and opinions." he shared, smiling.

"I know you're right, but I feel like my whole life has been about starting over."

"Again, that is life. I am not trying to minimize what you went through, but I don't want you to think your life is in ruins. Trust me, I worked on a house once that, to most people, appeared so condemned that nobody else thought it would ever be functional again. I believed otherwise, and today, it is one of the houses a family member of mine lives in. It's all about vision and seeing beyond the shit pile."

I laughed at that one. "Thank you so much for that visual."

Paul put the hammer in front of me again. "Are you going to remain demolished, or are you going to rebuild?"

I grabbed the hammer and held it up in the air. "I am going to rebuild! Damn it, I am going to rebuild!"

Paul took the hammer back and stated, "Now, that's what I am talking about! On that note, I need to run and pick up some items to finish this job tomorrow. I am really happy I ran into you, and proud of you for taking this step. You'll be fine, Knight. I have faith in you."

He gave me a hug and then went into his truck. I knocked on the side window. He rolled it down and grinned.

"Yes, Knight?"

"Thank you. Thank you for taking the time to care."

"People care, Knight. You just need to care enough about yourself. Keep on keeping on. I will see you soon."

Paul waved and backed out of the driveway. The sun was starting to set. Vibrant reds and pinks were taking over the sky at that moment. I felt like it was a sign that everything was going to be okay. Paul's words of wisdom hit me like an arrow in a jousting tournament, but this time I didn't fall off the horse. I remained in my position and vowed to stay that way no matter what.

Chapter 6

The next day was a busy, intense day. Renee was right; this computer program was very involved. I took tons of notes. She was encouraged by how I was able to take in a lot of what was presented and process it. I had told her that I am a visual learner, and this was the best way for me to be trained. She also showed me the email system and how new and established guests were already inquiring about reserving for the upcoming months. She made a remark about how there weren't as many as she had hoped, but didn't elaborate on it. I didn't press the issue.

"Opening day is extremely busy. In fact, I would like you to come in for a couple of hours that morning to observe Heather on the phone and how she checks in the guests. I will pay you for that time as well. I will be with you for the first couple of shifts. It's not that I feel you won't handle everything well, but trust me, it is a lot."

"That would be great. I don't mind. I want to do it all the right way."

"Tomorrow there is no training because I have to go out of town for the day, but you can go over your notes in the meantime. We will resume on Thursday."

"Sounds like a plan."

"How do you feel about everything so far?"

"It is all very interesting, but I am sure it is nothing like actually doing it for real."

"We have a lot of returning guests and families who come here every year. I don't like riff-raff, and I deal with it immediately. It's impossible to prevent every crazy scenario, but what I have done so far has worked for me."

"I saw on your site that you do breakfast on the weekends."

"Yes! Good point! Please bring that up on Thursday, and I will discuss that with you. I will also introduce you to some of the housekeeping staff and go over that as well."

"I can't wait!"

Renee thanked me for staying as long as I did that day and told me to enjoy my time off. I was looking forward to having a day to myself and mulling over everything that has taken place over this past week. As I was putting my jacket on, I heard my cell phone play a familiar tune. I wasn't going to pick it up, but I decided to at the last minute.

"Hello?"

"Well, it's nice to know you're still alive!"

"Yes, Gia, I haven't gotten swallowed up by the lake, yet."

Gia, which is short for Gianna, is a long-time friend whom I met at church. I love her to death, but she is obsessively bubbly, and I admit I haven't been in the mood for bubbly (except if you gave me a glass of champagne). In earlier years, I was a lot more like Gia, but when your heart is turned into shredded wheat, it just isn't happening.

"I have been texting you like crazy the past few days!"

"Yes, I know. My cell nearly blew up the other night and was begging for mercy."

I knew Gia was comfortable with my sometimes sarcastic sense of humor and I could get away with a remark like that to her.

"Ha-ha, funny. Forgive me for being so concerned about one of my best friends."

"I know, Gia, and I love you for that. I just wasn't in the mood for anybody's company, not just yours. Plus, I started a new job."

Now, this is another thing about Gia—she talks LOUD, no matter whether she is mad, glad, sad, or the like. She says it is because of her job as a creative arts therapist at local nursing homes, where she often has to shout to be heard. However, when she is shocked about something she gets much, much louder. I held the cell away from my head so I wouldn't end up with a busted eardrum. God forbid I put her on speakerphone; she would bring the apartment building down.

"WHAT???? SINCE WHEN?"

I was still holding the phone away from my ear. When she didn't hear anything from me, she yelled, "HELLO?"

I put the phone near me again and said, "Gia, you really need to go down a few decibels when you are on the phone. You just shattered all of my windows in the apartment."

"I know, sorry. It's a really bad habit of mine. I am so used to having to raise my voice for my job that it's become a part of me everywhere I go."

"If you were ever a ringmaster for a circus, you would not need a microphone or a megaphone."

"You know, that's not such a bad idea. Maybe in my next life I will do that."

That's Gia, the eternal optimist. Not that I meant my suggestion as an insult, and she would never take it like that anyway. Deep down, I admired her for who she was and wished that I could be like that again.

"Why don't we meet up for dinner and you can tell me all about your new job? And don't give me any 'you have plans' stuff. You just told me earlier you have been avoiding everybody."

"I will go out with you if you promise me that you will talk in a normal, acceptable voice and not start a battle that almost gets us kicked out of the restaurant like last time."

"Hey, it's not my fault that the table next to us had a bunch of screaming kids. What I had to say was important, and I was being drowned out by an argument over a stolen French fry."

I had to admit I could not argue that point, particularly when one of the fries came sailing past me like a missile. That was a no-no for Gia. Luckily the manager had mercy on us, especially when Gia ordered dessert and coffee for us both, providing more business for the place. On our way out, the manager reported other people complained about that particular table and were witnesses to the projectile French fries. I felt lucky to having escaped without injury.

"Okay," Gia announced, "I will try to watch my volume, but if we are seated anywhere near French fries, we look for another table."

"Deal."

Chapter 7

I was meeting Gia at 6 that evening. I was looking forward to seeing her. It is never boring when we get together, and she has been there for me consistently for the past several years. She has a serious boyfriend, who is just as positive and excited about life as she is. I keep asking her when they are going to get married and she always points to the sky when I ask.

"Whenever the dear Lord decides it's time."

"Uh…I think you two play a part in that."

"It will happen when the time is right."

I stopped asking Gia about her marriage plans a while ago, especially since it is a sensitive subject with me. It is ironic in a sense; she hasn't even begun that phase of her life, and my marriage had already ended. Life is strange in that way. Gia's boyfriend, Evan, is a wonderful soul who is very spiritual and wants the best for everyone, including me. When he heard what happened, he actually called me on his own and said how sorry he was and offered to help any way he could. It meant a lot.

I drove to one of our local favorite spots. Gia offered to treat me, which I told her wasn't necessary. She insisted, and I knew better than to argue with her. We were able to get seated right away.

"It's nice to see you among the land of the living again."

"It's tough, Gia."

"I know it is. That's why I was trying to get in touch with you so I could put some fun back in your life."

"Well, I appreciate it. I really do."

A female server came over to our table and asked what we wanted to drink. I asked for a Coke. Gia said if I wanted anything stronger I could, but my preference is to keep the order as cheap as possible when someone treats me. It could also be due to me having such a strict budget over the past few months that even a pizza was a luxury item. It was wonderful having a paycheck again.

"So tell me about this new job of yours! I've been in suspense!"

"Let's order first, then I will tell you."

Gia suggested we split an appetizer, and we agreed on nachos with some kind of fondue sauce. We both ordered burger platters for our meal. It may not be the healthiest meal in the world, but tonight was about pleasure and drowning sorrows in cheesy nachos and whatever else was available.

After our appetizer was delivered, I filled Gia in on my job at the Serenity Savor Motel. I told her about my day at the beach and the metal detector man. Gia smiled and waved a fork at me.

"See? I told you there are signs all over. I'm glad you recognized it."

"I work for a woman named Renee. She's been really great towards me. The training has been intense, but it fills the time."

"Well, it all sounds terrific. You think you'll like it?"

"Time will tell. So far I do. I had to do something, Gia. The best is I have no commute."

"Well, aren't you lucky! I think you will do fantastic, if you want my opinion."

As I was dipping a nacho into piping hot fondue, someone came up to our table and called out, "Is that you, Sage?"

I looked up and suddenly felt a huge knot in my stomach. Gia must have sensed something was up because she kept her eyes focused on me.

"Hi, Kayla."

"I wanted to tell you how sorry I am about your break-up."

At that point, Gia's fork would have felt less painful even if she stabbed me in the heart with it. Gia's eyes closed, and she shook her head slightly.

"Thank you, Kayla." I said, going back to my food. I hope she got the message that I wasn't interested in pursuing this conversation any further. No such luck.

"Are you okay?" She asked. The way she said it, it almost sounded like she was mocking me.

I felt tears come to my eyes. Before I could say anything, Gia intervened and stated, "Sage is terrific. In fact, we are celebrating her new position as a reservations specialist at a local lodging area. Her boss saw how wonderful of a person and employee she is, AND appreciates her."

The inferences were not lost on Kayla. I managed to look directly at Kayla and nodded my head in agreement. Kayla looked almost annoyed that she couldn't get a reaction from me, so she walked away without saying anything further.

"Maybe this was a bad idea." I said, starting to collect my purse and keys.

"Sage, no! Do NOT give her the satisfaction. I am sure she is watching you at this very moment just dying to see what you will do. Just keep on eating those nachos like you were before."

As hard as it was, I remained at the table. My stomach still felt queasy, though. After a few minutes, Gia asked, "Who was that broad anyway?"

"I don't want to talk about it, Gia. Let's just forget that it happened."

Gia knew full well that I wasn't about to forget what just happened, but she did not comment any further.

"Reservations Specialist? Local lodging area?"

"Hey, it's all true, right? You're doing reservations and do work at local lodging. Be proud of what you are doing. It's still God's work no matter how you look at it."

The rest of our food arrived, and I have to say I was enjoying myself. Gia always manages to spin the positive web no matter where we are. Kayla walked by our table again, probably on the way to the ladies' room, but she ignored us this time.

"I hope she falls in." Gia blurted out.

"Gia! This, out of your mouth?" I scolded.

"Hey, I'm human! She hurt my best friend, and that's a no-no with me."

"Thanks for the visual, though." I did manage a smile.

We were at the restaurant for over three hours. Gia and I split a big piece of carrot cake for dessert. By the time we left, I was feeling better than I had in months. Gia walked me to my car.

"I can't thank you enough for tonight. I didn't realize how much I needed a night out."

"I'm so sorry that woman upset you earlier."

"Forget about it, Gia. Unfortunately, it's a reality for me. I still had a great time regardless."

"You'll have to come over to my house soon for dinner. Evan asked about you the other day. We can do dinner and a movie all in the comfort of my condo."

"It sounds wonderful. I will let you know. Thanks so much again."

Gia gave me a big hug.

"I love you, BFF. You need anything, you know where to find me. And respond to your text messages more often."

"I love you too. I will talk to you soon. Give my love to Evan. And tell him to marry you soon!"

"From your mouth to God's ears."

I watched Gia get into her own car and start it before I left to go home. I made a mental note to myself to reach out to her tomorrow and thank her again for such a fun time, and for believing in me.

Chapter 8

The day was here: opening day at the motel. I barely slept the night before due to nerves. I woke up at six and had two cups of tea. Hopefully there will be coffee at the motel for extra caffeine.

Heather and I agreed for me to come in around seven-thirty that morning so she could go over some procedures before the phone calls began at eight. I had met the housekeeping staff and they were all nice and welcoming to me. Renee felt I was as prepared as I could be, but now it was time to put it to the test. At least I was just an observer this morning and Renee agreed to work with me today and tomorrow. After this weekend I would be working Friday and Saturday nights from 3 to 11 and gradually increasing to more shifts as the summer approached. Since she opened this Saturday, Renee asked me to work 3 to 6 tomorrow for extra training.

Heather was already at the desk by the time I arrived at 7:25 AM.

"Hey, Sage! Welcome to opening day! Go grab yourself a coffee over there. There is no breakfast this morning since nobody was here last night, but I made coffee for us. It's going to be crazy once eight hits. Actually, the phones may start before then."

No sooner did she say that, and the phone did ring.

"Go get your coffee while I answer this. Trust me, there will be a lot to see and hear today."

I walked over to the breakfast bar area and helped myself to coffee. It was a nice little set-up. Renee told me that one of the duties as a night shift worker was to make sure the breakfast bar was set up for the next morning, with the exception of the food and beverage items, and the coffee maker was set to begin perking at 6:00 AM. The day clerk put the bagels out along with the milk, creamer, butter and cream cheese. Renee also offered some breakfast pastries in a separate basket. Another one of my duties would be to help out with doing laundry with the motel linens, but that would be later down the road when more guests would be staying. Heather was still on the phone when I walked back to the desk area, so I sat down and sipped my coffee until she was done.

"Your coffee tastes fantastic!" I stated when she finally hung up the phone.

"Thank you. It's survival for me at times. So, that call was from one of our regulars. He wants our biggest room with the king bed for his stay in July, and does not want to miss out."

"I guess you get a lot of that, huh?"

"Oh my God, yes. I understand, though. It's one of the nicest rooms here and it's very popular."

I spent a lot of time getting to know the locations and details of each room at the motel as part of my training. Renee and Heather were very impressed with how I memorized a lot of what I took in. I stated that it was my saving grace in college.

For the next two hours I observed Heather on the phone. I was amazed at how many phone calls came in that morning. That proverbial knot showed up in my stomach again as I thought, *can I really handle this?* Heather made it look easy. I had a notebook with me and was busy jotting notes down whenever I thought something would help me. I was writing so much that I thought I was going to fill the book in one shift!

At 11:15AM, a man walked in the lobby and over to the desk. I was sitting in the chair opposite where Heather was, and she happened to be on the phone. The man walked over to where I was sitting.

"Hi there, miss."

"Hello." I responded.

"Do you work here?"

I caught Heather signaling that she would attend to him as soon as she got off the phone, but I did not want to appear rude, so I stood up and said, "Yes, I do. Actually, I am new here and this is my first day at the front desk. Heather will be able to check you in as soon as she is done with her phone call with another guest."

The man thanked me for the information and headed over to where Heather was. The sweat was pouring off of me from anxiety. Heather took care of the man who happened to be a walk-in for an overnight stay. When he left the lobby, Heather turned to me and stated, "I happened to hear what you said to that guest when I was on the phone. That was awesome how you handled that. Very professional, and he did not feel put off."

"Thank you for saying that, I was nervous."

"You'll be fine, don't be so hard on yourself. This is a fun job, for the most part." She added, winking.

Easier said than done, I thought. I knew she was trying to put me at ease and I really appreciated it.

The rest of the morning went pretty smoothly, except for one guest who called down to the desk that his refrigerator wasn't working. When she asked him if it was plugged in, I stared at her thinking, *REALLY?* It turned out that was the issue after all. Heather laughed and stated that sometimes the appliances get unplugged and until it is brought to our attention no one would know. I shook my head.

"I would feel ridiculous in even asking something like that!" I admitted.

"Sometimes the silliest question is the most logical one. Trust me, after a few weeks you will be used to it."

I hung around until noon and told Heather I would be back before 3PM. Heather said I did well and that she appreciated my help, and I left there feeling a lot less nervous than I did earlier. Perhaps I really can do this. I just need to keep believing it.

Chapter 9

2:35 pm. This is it. In twenty-five minutes, I will be an official front desk clerk at the Serenity Savor Motel. I will officially be the night shift worker. Gia sent me a text earlier wishing me blessings and fun for my first real shift, and required (yes, required) a detailed update the next day. As intense as Gia can be sometimes, no one has my back like she does. If I was in serious trouble and no one else could be there, Gia would knock down a concrete wall with her bare hands to get to me. That kind of friendship is priceless these days.

I ate lunch at my apartment before I needed to go back to work. Renee and Heather said it was okay to eat at the desk, but I wanted to get the lay of the land first. All I need is to be eating a sandwich at the desk and welcome guests with a poppy seed stuck in the middle of my teeth. That happened to me one day when I was teaching, and the kids were very quick to point it out to me. One of the boys even thought it was a bug. Anyway, lesson learned.

At 2:45PM I headed over to the motel. Heather was writing on a gold envelope.

"Hi! Great timing! I can show you the drawer and how to count it out for the next shift."

Heather showed me the procedure. It seemed a little complicated at first, but a lot was appearing that way. The drawer came out even.

"That's because I wasn't on duty yet." I half-joked. Heather just gave me a look and shook her head.

"The phones have calmed down a bit. You may have a couple more walk-ins, but my Mom will be training you tonight."

"I appreciate everything you have shown me today."

"I appreciate you working here. You will be great, I can tell."

I wish I had her confidence. No sooner did I think that, and both lines started ringing at the same time. Heather was able to manage answering both, putting one on hold while dealing with the other, and then going back to the second caller. She did say that it was okay to let it go to voicemail if needed, but she preferred acknowledging each caller. I picked up Line 1 and went ahead with my greeting. I also noticed Line 2 was picked up by someone else. When I hung up Heather explained to me that often her mother will pick up the second line in the back office, especially if there are people at the desk. Heather grabbed her cell phone, a notebook, and a half-finished bottle of water and started towards the house door.

"Relax! You'll be fine!"

"I just don't want to mess up." I admitted.

"Do you have one of those perfectionistic personalities? Let me tell you, it will drive you insane. My last boyfriend was all about that, and it drove me crazy. He could never let loose, and then he expected it of me. I don't have time for that shit. What you see is what you get with me."

The bluntness out of Heather surprised me at first, but I had to admit that it had a ring of truth to it. I am always hard on myself, but with good reason. Not that she knew anything about my crazy past. And then, as if she could read my mind Heather stated, "Sorry, I probably sounded a bit harsh. It's none of my business, and I don't know you or where you came from. I guess it comes from being a bartender and hearing pity parties and sob stories all the time."

"You're a bartender too?"

"Yes. That's another reason I work the day shift. I bartend four nights a week. I am actually applying to go into a hospitality program beginning next winter. Mom is a bit bummed about it because she wants me here, but between you and me, I have even bigger dreams. I want to get into a big chain hotel and work in the food and beverage operation. I also want to move to the city. The lake is beautiful, but I crave the city life."

"I can understand that. I lived in Philadelphia for a year. I loved it."

"Why did you move back?"

"It was a paid-volunteer job that ended."

"Ahh, gotcha. We should hang out one night when you aren't working here and you can fill me in on what Philly life was like. I am also looking into New York City or Boston."

"Sounds like a plan."

The phone rang again, and Heather waved. For the next hour, I mainly dealt with people inquiring about Memorial Weekend. At one point, I felt a lot calmer than when I first came in. When I had a little break with the phones, I reflected on the conversation I had with Heather earlier. First, I admired her work ethic and second,

I loved how goal-oriented she was. I could definitely see her at a big year-round hotel. I also thought about how I came across to her. It was a bit of a jolt to realize how negative and jaded I have become. That was not always the case.

Renee came out around 6:00PM and asked how I was doing. I told her I had quite a few phone calls which were without incident, and I even checked in two families and one couple.

"That's great! I had no doubt that you would do well."

"It's very different from being in the classroom, that's for sure."

"Do you think you will ever go back to that?"

"I don't really see it at this point." I answered honestly.

"Well, their loss, my gain."

That comment touched my heart. When Renee went back into the house, I glanced at the room roster. I still had one person to check in, a male guest. I began to relax. I walked around the lobby and took in the views outside. The sun was setting, and the temperature was a lot cooler. I brought a sweater with me in case it got too cold inside. I saw some people walking around the beach area, where I was just over two months ago contemplating the direction of my life. As I have always been told, you just never know what the future holds. I heard the phone ringing, so I dashed back to the desk to answer it. In my haste, I knocked over my notebook and a couple of pens. I took the call, which was a rate question concerning the following weekend. Renee referred to them as "lookie-loos." After I hung up with the caller, I bent down to pick up the items that landed on the floor. What happened next, I could have never predicted.

Chapter 10

When I stood back up, I realized it was a waste of time to pick everything back up because it all wound up flying across the lobby after what I saw. A clown (yes, a real live circus-looking Bozo) was standing right in front of the counter. I never even heard any footsteps or a door opening. I screamed, and my notebook and pens decided to grow wings. It made me think of Gia's French fry incident. *Geez, what is it with me and things becoming missiles in my presence?* I wondered. Renee must have heard my scream because she came bursting out of the house with a giant frying pan in her hands. When she saw Clown Dude (or Dudette), she instantly relaxed.

"I must be losing my touch." It was definitely Clown Dude.

"Derek, you scared my new desk clerk to death!"

"Uh…how about the ol' cast iron there?" He was pointing at the black frying pan. "I was pretty close to death myself."

"I thought she was getting attacked!"

"Um, can someone please explain to the third person here what is going on?" I asked. One of my biggest pet peeves is when people talk about you like you are not even in the room, though you are clearly right there.

"Sorry," Clown Dude Derek stated. "I am Derek Diminno, otherwise known as Minno the Clown."

"I like it."

"I feel so bad scaring you like that. I thought Heather would be on, and she has seen me in costume already."

"No, she was here earlier. I am the new night shift girl, Sage Knight."

"Sage Knight working the night shift. Awesome!"

I grinned to myself because I never made the connection until he said that. Renee opened the door to her house and stated, "Well, now that I know my staff and motel are safe, I am going to resume making my omelet."

"Your famous everything omelet?" Derek questioned.

"Yes. Sometimes there is nothing like breakfast for dinner. Derek, it's great to have you back."

"Same here, Ms. Renee."

I could not wait to tell Gia about this! I haven't checked my cell since I began my shift. She probably left five million text messages by now wondering how things were going.

"So were you in a parade today or doing a kids' party?" I asked Derek.

"I work here for the season actually. I begin with weekends, and then by Memorial Day, I am working practically seven days a week. I perform all over, especially on some of the boat cruises. I stay only at Serenity Savor."

I extended my hand to make up for a proper greeting. "I am so sorry for overreacting like that."

Derek laughed. "Hey, if I suddenly stood up and saw myself standing over the desk…well, you were a lot more gracious than I would have been."

I went to check Derek in, but truthfully, it was very hard to keep a straight face with a clown standing in front of you. I know a lot of people have had bad experiences with them, but I actually have some nice memories of clowns from circuses and my high school youth group. I processed all of the paperwork and handed him his room key.

"Wow, that was quick! You're good." Derek seemed genuinely impressed.

"Not bad for first day on the job, huh?"

"I am going to change out of Minno, and then you can meet the real Derek."

"I'll be here."

For some unexplained reason, I felt a considerable calm around Derek. Even in costume, and after the initial shock of seeing him, he exuded warmth and caring. Renee stepped out of the house to check on me.

"Have you recovered yet?"

"Yes, thanks. Oh my God, that was crazy at first. He seems very nice, though."

"He is. He does a lot for the kids and families around here, especially in the summer. The boat cruise staff love him."

"He said he only stays at Serenity Savor. Is that true?"

Renee nodded. "Heather and I talk about it constantly. We have no idea where he gets all of his money from. He has said over time that God has blessed him through many means, and he has a lot of businesses going. We have never had one issue with him, and he has been staying here for three years now. He pays on time, and his room is immaculate. Rayna often says that it is like he never even stays in there."

Rayna is the head housekeeper. She is an amazing woman who can do everything in my book. She is a single mother who has related to a lot of what I have been dealing with concerning my marriage break-up. She has five-year-old twins (a boy and a girl), and they are absolutely adorable.

"Have you eaten yet? I can make you an omelet."

I was taken aback by the offer. "I don't want to put you through any trouble."

"It is no trouble at all. I love to cook. I have dreams one day of opening a bed and breakfast, possibly even converting this place. My husband Keith and I have even discussed buying something near the ski lodge where he works. I know Heather is going to move to the city at some point because she wants to work in a big hotel."

"She mentioned that to me earlier when she told me about her bartending job. That must make you sad, if you don't mind me saying."

Renee shook her head. "At first it did, but Heather has a totally different personality than I do. Heather loves crowds, energy, and a lot of activity all at once. She thrives on it, actually. Her boss at the Paddlewheel loves her. This summer she is going to be the evening shift bar manager, and she is thrilled! I am very proud of her."

The Paddlewheel is a local bar that is very popular with the locals and tourists. Gia and I had gone last summer to watch a band play, and we had a great time. The food is awesome there as well.

Renee continued, "I, on the other hand, love the atmosphere of smaller lodging. I enjoy getting to know my guests and being more personal. Not that you can't be personal at a bigger hotel, but I just prefer it this way. Anyway, enough of my rambling. Let me make you that omelet. Are you allergic to any foods?"

"Nope. I can eat anything, which can be a blessing and a curse."

Renee chuckled. "I know what you mean."

I thought about what Renee shared. Deep down, I was envious of Heather. I was always the shy kid. Crowds always scared me. I was a loner most of my life, but I don't really resent it. I have fond memories of the swing set my father put up for me. I would be on that swing for hours and hours. Even having to pee did not deter me, though I learned that lesson the hard way. I had a very vivid imagination, and I could create scenarios in my mind that kept me entertained more than the kids at my school could. I was not a popular kid. In fact, I was bullied a lot. *Ugh, not something I really want to think about right now,* I thought. So, I took out my cell phone to check my messages. Gia did not disappoint. There were at least fifteen texts from her wondering how things were going (good thing I have unlimited messaging as part of my plan), and two voicemails. The first was from my parents, and the second message was one I was not prepared for.

Chapter 11

The message began with "Hi, Sager." One person in my entire life only called me Sager—my older sister. The sister whom none of us have heard from in years. I had to listen to the message a couple of times because I was in such disbelief that I was hearing her voice.

"Are you okay, miss?"

I jumped because I did not realize I had someone standing at the front desk. Then I immediately felt embarrassed. I shoved my cell phone in one of the drawers and attended to the person in front of me. I apologized for being distracted. Thank goodness he was fine with it, but I mentally beat myself up for letting that phone call upset me. All the guest wanted was some extra plastic cups, which I retrieved for him. Five minutes later, Renee stepped out with a plate that contained the biggest omelet I have ever seen. I mean, this was an omelet that would have satisfied Paul Bunyan. She also included two pieces of rye toast. Renee put the plate down on the counter, but when she took a look at me, she appeared concerned.

"Are you all right, Sage?"

"Yes, why?"

"You're white as a ghost. Even worse than when Derek scared you earlier."

Great, now I would get a reputation for being a fraidy cat. I was not going to get into the situation about my sister. Not even Gia knows that part of my history, and she is one of my closest friends ever.

"Low blood sugar. It's a good thing you made me this omelet because I am feeling a bit dizzy. This is huge!"

"Well, I figured this being your first day and all, you deserved a treat. I hope you feel better, let me know if you need anything." She said. Renee really seemed to care about my well-being. It's definitely not what I have been used to.

So, this is the famous omelet that Derek was referring to earlier, I thought, eyeballing it. After my first bite, I thought I died and went to food heaven. This was amazeballs! Of course, a man had to walk in at the exact time, but it was ironic because it was Derek.

"Ahh, she made you the omelet!"

"Oh my gosh, this is insane, it's so good!"

'I'm jealous!" he joked.

"I think Renee took pity on me because it's my first day, and you almost gave me a heart attack." I winked when I said that.

"I still feel bad about that. Hey, you feeling okay? You look pale."

Jeez, what was this, the face color police? Did I really look THAT bad? I better put on extra blush tomorrow in case of any additional shocks to the system. I thought.

"Just low blood sugar. Renee came to my rescue."

He seemed to buy it, like Renee did. I took in Derek's physical features. He was a really good-looking guy. Dark brown hair, blue eyes, and just enough bulk. Again, I felt that peace and calm when he walked into the lobby.

"I am running to the store to pick up a few things. Can I bring you back anything?"

"Oh no, I am good. Thank you, though."

"You sure?"

"Yes. I appreciate it, though."

"See you later, Sager."

I almost collapsed. I had to steady myself, or I would have fallen down. Based on today's events maybe the computer should be placed on the floor.

"What did you say?"

Derek turned around. "What?"

"You just called me Sager."

Derek quickly walked back to the desk. This time I could not hide the anguish in my face and eyes. He came around to the back of the desk and held onto my arm.

"Come on over here and sit on the chair."

I didn't argue with him. He was so calm and gentle. I was having trouble breathing. He sat in front of me and encouraged me to breathe slowly and deeply. He kept his hand on my arm the whole time. Finally, I was back to breathing normally again.

"Thank you. You must think I'm a basket case."

"Not at all. I just seem to keep upsetting you when I don't mean to."

"It's not your fault. And you would have no way of knowing why the name Sager would affect me like that. It's okay, though."

"I was just making up a rhyme, like see you later, alligator. I just added an r to your name. So sorry."

I shook my head. "Again, not your fault. There is just something very sad attached to that name for me, but it's fine."

"I think this calls for a hot chocolate."

Derek stayed with me until I maneuvered back to the desk. Then, he announced he would bring me back a hot chocolate from the local market. I did not argue with him. At this point, he could spike it with something and I wouldn't care. I went back to my omelet and toast. Damn, why did that call have to come today, of all days? Here I am trying to begin a new job, and all hell is breaking loose.

I heard another ping from the drawer, which indicated a text. Probably Gia again. She is most likely up to thirty text messages by now. I better respond, or she will send the National Guard in to check on me. I wrote back that everything is fine (yeah, stretching the truth a bit), and that I had a lot to tell her. I also wrote that I would touch base with her tomorrow morning. Within two minutes, she responded back by thanking me for letting her know I was still alive, and that she would look forward to my call tomorrow morning. I grinned. She is a faithful friend.

Believe it or not, the rest of the night went smoothly. Derek brought back my hot chocolate (non-spiked), which was delicious, and he talked a lot about his clown adventures. He was very entertaining to listen to. A couple of his stories had me in stitches. Before I left for the night, I prepared the breakfast buffet and set the coffee up. I prayed I did everything right. I even got to meet Renee's husband Keith before I left. He was nice and very athletic-looking. He said he had aspirations of becoming an Olympic skier but then he met Renee, fell in love, and the rest was history. He loves teaching people how to ski, especially children. You could tell how in love they still were with each other. *Must be nice*, I thought.

Derek hung around until I locked up for the night. Renee told me before I left that I did a fantastic job and how happy she was that she hired me. I thanked her for her belief in me, and told her that I really enjoyed the work. Derek offered to walk with me back to my apartment. I told him it wasn't necessary, but he insisted. It was very dark so I thought it would be a good idea. When I put the key in the lock, he apologized again for upsetting me earlier with the nickname.

"It's okay. Really, it is. To be honest…I received a phone call from someone before you came in who is associated with that name. This person is the only one who ever called me Sager."

Derek nodded. "I get it. Wow, no wonder you reacted the way you did. Well, I won't make that mistake again."

"Actually, this is crazy, but…I wouldn't mind if you did. Maybe it will help me deal better with what happened."

"Sure, as long as you're okay with it."

"I am."

"Okay then, Sager it is. I won't see you until tomorrow evening. I have a full day of Minno work."

"Have fun!"

Derek walked back to the motel, and I flopped down in my lounger. I made it through my first shift! I was so exhausted, more mentally than physically. I was still trying to process the phone call from Kendra, my long-lost sister. I can't believe I opened up to Derek about the phone call, but I felt comfortable enough to do it. What really amazed me was that Derek didn't press me for details. It's almost like he knew I wasn't ready to talk about it. I took out my cell phone and stared at it. Kendra gave me a pre-paid cell number to call, but she said it wasn't hers so someone else may pick up first. I am amazed she even had my number still. She said I could call her anytime. I stared some more. Was I ready for this? I haven't heard from my sister for nearly ten years. Did she reach out to Mom and Dad too? *Oh, what the heck* I thought. I called the number she provided. After four rings, a very groggy, male voice answered, "Yeah?"

I cleared my throat, wondering if I dialed the right number, and practically whispered, "Um… hi. Is Kendra available?"

"Yeah, she's here. Calling a bit late, aren't ya?" The voice wasn't that friendly.

"I just got off work." I said a little defensively.

"Sager, is that you?"

At that moment, time stood still. My head went to another dimension. I feel like I woke up out of a long coma and heard familiar voices for the first time. It was like an emotional archaeological discovery embedded in the heart. There was my sister, her voice so close, but she was so far away. She had been for years.

"Kendra…" was all I could manage to say.

I heard deep sobbing on the other end. Then a voice in the background that said angrily, "If you're gonna do all that crying shit, go in the other room. I need to sleep. I thought you were done with those people anyway."

Those people? Nice company my sister was keeping. After a brief silent moment, Kendra came back on the line.

"Sorry about that. Glen has to get up at 5:00AM for work. He's a security guard."

"Kendra, where are you? And why are you with someone so mean?"

"You know I can't tell you that. And Glen isn't mean. You woke him up by calling so late. It's after 11:30PM, for Pete's sake!"

I was beginning to lose patience. "I started a new job today, okay? I work the night shift, 3 to 11. You said I could call anytime, so that was your fault. You should have been more specific with your time constraints!"

"I see you still use the big words. Going for your Ph.D yet?" Kendra asked in a snotty way.

What was going on with Kendra? One minute she's bawling from hearing my voice, and now she's attacking me.

"Kendra, you called me. Are you okay?"

She softened again. "I just…I don't know. I was in a store this morning, and some woman mentioned she was buying sage. It made me think of you."

"Did you call Mom and Dad?"

She snorted. "Are you kidding me? I'm sure you'll tell them you talked to me first thing tomorrow morning."

"Not necessarily. I don't want to upset them. It's hard enough for them dealing with my divorce."

Kendra didn't speak for a minute. "I didn't even know you got married."

"Yeah, you've missed a lot."

It was a cheap shot, but at that point I didn't care. I was tired, and I didn't want to get into anything further with her. Suddenly, I heard a booming voice yell out, "Kendra! Get off the damn phone! I have to go to work in a few hours!"

"Just another minute!" she shouted back.

What happened next absolutely stabbed and ripped apart my heart. I heard slamming footsteps, the phone falling on the floor, a whimper, and then a horrible slap. Next was my sister crying even worse than before. I heard Glen clearly say, "You…don't…ever talk back to me like that. You hear me?" With that, I heard another slap, and I yelled into the phone, "Stop hurting my sister, you big jerk!"

I was positively fuming with rage. Glen grabbed the phone and yelled, "Don't ever call this number again, you understand me? Kendra was under control until your name came up! I keep her in line! She left you and your family for a reason. Leave us alone!"

With that, the line went dead. I can only imagine what Kendra was going through right now. In some ways I felt guilty because I made the call. Why did Kendra call me in the first place and tell me to reach out to her? And what did Glen mean when he said she left us for a reason? Nothing made sense. I was shaking to death. I wish I had someone to talk to, but it was nearly midnight. I got on my knees and said a prayer for Kendra. There was nothing more I could do.

Chapter 12

The next day I got up feeling like a truck ran over me, minus the alcohol. To be honest, I barely slept. I had nightmares of what was happening to my sister. I kept hearing the slapping sounds over and over. I felt sick to my stomach, but there was nothing else I could do. Glen probably ditched the phone and got a new one. I couldn't tell my parents; they would be heartbroken. I heard my phone ringing. I recognized the ringtone as Gia's.

"Hello." I said, barely audible.

"Geez, you sound hungover." Gia never sugar-coated anything.

"No, just a sleepless night. I think it was first day on the job jitters."

"Uh, usually you get those before you start a new job."

"I had those too."

"Soooo…how was it?"

I filled her in on everything that happened, minus the trauma with Kendra. I couldn't process all of that yet. Gia absolutely lost it when I filled her in on Derek showing up at the desk in clown costume. She said she wished she was a fly on the wall when that happened. She also came up with the idea of having him perform at the nursing homes that she works out of. Then Gia, the eternal optimist and romantic, comes out with, "So, do you think he likes you?"

"Of course. He's a clown. He likes everybody."

"You know what I mean!" Gia stated.

"Yes, Gia, I know exactly what you mean. First, I just met him, and you know I am not looking for anybody to date."

"Yeah, but you could have a lot of fun with costumes and stuff…"

"Gia!" I yelled, my face turning red. "Where your mind goes to sometimes."

She laughed. "Yeah, I know. Evan is worse sometimes, if you can believe that."

I didn't, but I wasn't about to argue the point. Gia then informed me she and Evan were going to a movie later. I told her that I was working tonight and wouldn't be off until next Friday night.

Gia and I promised to get together at some point during the week, and then we hung up. I was still restless from the chaos last night, and my stomach was rumbling. I had to restock on groceries but I wasn't in the mood to go today, especially on a Sunday morning. Sometimes you took your life in your hands when attempting to go food shopping on the first day of weekly sales. I have battle scars on my ankles from carts banging into me.

I glanced at my phone. I still had a few hours before my shift began and I wanted to go for a walk. I decided to take a trip to one of the cafes that remained open all year. I was in the mood for a big, greasy breakfast sandwich and a steaming cup of coffee. I needed to regroup from Kendra's call. I grabbed my latest mystery novel and headed out the door.

The Hungry Laker Café is one of my favorite spots to eat. They know me by name, but I am affectionately referred to as the Book Lady. *Well, if I am alone, why not?* I figured. I am surely not going to talk to myself, at least not in public anyway. A few months ago, a couple came into the café and wanted my particular table. The woman made a comment that I was reading a book. *Thank you, Captain Obvious,* I mentioned in my head after hearing her request. After five minutes, she stated slowly, "And she's still reading." I caught a glance with the hostess, whom I adored. She was subtly grinning. Truth be known, I was about ready to pack it up, but I was tempted to read at least ten more pages. Rather than let this couple explode by spontaneous combustion I left a tip, picked up my book, and sauntered right by them. When Ally, the hostess, asked me how my breakfast was, I said with an elevated voice, "Great, but I didn't realize there were assigned seats in this cafe." With that, Ally turned around because she was trying so hard not to laugh. I paid my bill and couldn't help myself by pointing out, "I guess it's a good thing I wasn't reading Moby Dick." Ally's face turned nearly purple because she did not want to burst into laughter in front of the couple, who by then moved to another area of the café. When I went back to Hungry Laker a week later, Ally came running up to me and said, "Oh my God, I nearly peed my pants last week when you were here with that couple wanting your table! When you said the thing about Moby Dick, I nearly fell over! You are too much!" I have always been told I have a wonderful sense of humor, but it often gets mixed up with some sarcasm along the way. Survival skills, I guess.

I could smell the amazing aromas from Hungry Laker a block away. I noticed the town was starting to fill up a little more with tourists. The weather was getting warmer, and the mountains were all decked out in lush greenery. I never get tired of that view. Memorial Weekend was approaching, and both Heather and

Renee kept repeating how busy they hoped it would be at the motel. My hours would start increasing next month, too. I was looking forward to the extra money.

Ally was behind the front counter and waved to me when I came in.

"Hey, there's my favorite customer!"

I smiled and blushed at the same time. Ally brought me a menu and led me to a small table. Normally I order the special of two eggs done any style (over easy), choice of meat (bacon), grits, toast (rye), juice (apple), and decaf coffee; this morning I went with the sausage, egg, and cheese on a bagel platter. After last night's events, I needed this! The price was amazing, along with the food. I opened my book to the last page I was on.

"So what are you reading now?"

I showed her the book by one of my favorite female authors. Ally nodded her approval.

"You think anyone has their teeth set on this table this morning?" I asked, winking at her.

"Oh my gosh, don't get me started laughing again! It took me a week to recover from that whole scenario. Even the owner loved the story!"

It was a good thing because I would not have wanted to be banned from here. Ally sent the server over and once I ordered, I began to read. I was so engrossed in the novel that I didn't hear the front door open. Next thing I knew, a shadow loomed over me. I looked up to see Derek standing over me wearing a bright red clown nose.

"Really, Derek?"

"Well, I figured this wasn't as scary as the whole costume."

I playfully hit him with my napkin. "You are never going to let me live that one down, are you?"

"Actually, I always carry a red nose around in case the moment arises. I happened to see you come here earlier, so it was one of those moments."

I shook my head, grinning. He definitely made me laugh, which I secretly needed. At that point, my breakfast arrived.

"Are you harassing our customers, Minno?" Wendy, my server, asked kiddingly.

"It's fine." I assured Wendy. "I know him from where I work."

"You behave yourself, especially with that!" she exclaimed, tapping a finger on the red nose.

"Would you like to sit down?" I offered.

"Are you sure? You look like you are in the middle of a hot story." he said, indicating the book. I shut it and offered my hand to the seat opposite me.

"It's no problem, I can read anytime."

Derek took me up on it and wound up ordering his own breakfast. He loved omelets, so he ordered the vegetable one along with wheat toast, orange juice, and decaf coffee. I looked down at my breakfast sandwich feeling guilty.

"Don't worry about it. I just prefer omelets."

How does he always seem to know exactly what I am thinking?

"Unfortunately, food is my coping mechanism. Always has been."

"Ah, don't beat yourself up. The food is awesome around here. Enjoy it."

It's so bizarre how Derek happened to show up this particular morning. Of course, I did not fill him in about Kendra, but it was really comforting to have him there. We wound up talking a lot about how we got into certain careers. I shared with him about losing my teaching job due to illness. Derek asked me if I intended on going back into the field.

"That's funny, because Renee asked me the same thing. I really don't think so. I had two experiences that didn't work out. It wasn't the kids, like most expect. It was some of the adults."

Derek nodded in support. "Usually is, that's why I like working solo. I can yell at myself, but nobody else has that permission."

His comment made me think about Kendra. "I wish it were that simple."

"It can be. You just need to believe you are the whole breakfast sandwich and not just the homefries, though they are sooo good here!"

I sat back and shook my head. He definitely pursued the right profession for himself.

"I really like working at the motel. I enjoy meeting the guests, and I love Renee and Heather."

"Have you met Keith yet?" He asked, referring to Renee's husband.

"Yes, I have. He is fantastic too. He told me that during the spring and summer he is going to help Renee with the pool and other maintenance. They are so close-knit."

"Renee certainly deserves it. She hasn't had an easy time of it, especially now that the motel is hurting financially."

I spit out the coffee that was sloshing away in my mouth.

"What? What are you talking about?"

"Oh my gosh, Renee hasn't told you?"

"No! And now that you mentioned it, you better fill me in."

Derek nodded. "Okay, but not here. Let's go for a walk to the lake."

Chapter 13

Derek and I were sitting on a bench attached to the pier located by one of the little lake beaches. The tour cruise steamboats were performing test runs in preparation for the new season. I loved these boats, and my family and I have often taken the cruises. So did someone else in my life, but that is for another time.

Derek insisted on paying for my breakfast, even though I told him it wasn't necessary. He said it was compensation for dropping that bombshell on me, and the projectile coffee. There were a couple of families lolling on the beach but they were out of earshot from our conversation.

"Okay, we are alone now. What is going on with Serenity Savor?"

Derek took a deep breath.

"When I made my reservations for this year, I could just tell that something was bothering Renee. I could hear it in her voice."

Just like with me. He should be a clown/psychologist.

"Since Renee and I have a long history, I flat out asked her what was wrong. She actually started to cry on the phone. I told her to say no more, that I was coming to see her in person. So I did."

I always thought Gia had the biggest heart of anyone I ever knew, but Derek was close to surpassing that.

"We met up one day when her husband was working, and Heather was at the Paddlewheel. She just lost it. I guess being a clown has its benefits. People feel comfortable enough to spill their guts to you."

"Your compassionate spirit also helps." I pointed out.

Derek grinned at that. "Gosh, thank you. I try. Well, Renee admitted that over the last few years the amount of guests staying at her motel has been steadily declining. She spoke with other friends in the area who own lodging, and their numbers were higher. She was really discouraged after those conversations. Renee admitted to me that marketing is not her strong suit, and she took it for granted that people would just show up. Heather has tried to help, but she basically stated to her mother that she wants to work in the bigger hotels and live in the city. Plus, she has this new responsibility of evening bar manager. Her husband normally works at the ski lodge in other capacities, but to save money for Renee, he worked something out with the lodge owner where he would primarily work at the motel during the summer until next ski season."

I shook my head in disbelief. "I had absolutely no clue that this was all going on. I feel terrible for all of them. I am shocked that she even hired a new desk clerk."

"She needed to. That was another issue, which she thinks added to the declining numbers. The woman she previously employed was not very nice with the guests at times and, in my opinion, had zero personality for the job. She was fast and efficient, but in the hospitality business, attitude shines above the rest. Between you and me, Renee loves you. She believes you were sent to her."

I got a chill at that comment. I have a very strong faith in God, but I don't know if I was actually sent to Renee. Besides my demeanor, I don't feel I have very much to offer.

"I wish she would have told me all of this."

"She doesn't want to scare you away, plus Renee is very private when it comes to her personal life. Heather, on the other hand, is an open book. I know the Paddlewheel owner is aware of the situation, which I believe is one reason he offered Heather the promotion. This is in strictest confidence---Heather isn't taking a salary for her desk job. That is her way of helping her mom. She knows how much Serenity Savor means to Renee, so she is willing to sacrifice her pay."

Tears came to my eyes. What an amazing family. I had a new profound respect for all of them.

"I wish I could do more to help them. I just don't know what."

"Are you a praying woman?"

I was thrown a bit by that question. I looked at Derek and stated, "Yes, I am. Why?"

Derek stood up. "Because now that you know the truth, ask God how he can use you."

"I never worked in this profession. I don't know what else I can do."

He cupped his chin. "Ask Him. Just be open to how He responds. Now, I need to get ready for my work today. I am leaving tonight. I will be back next weekend."

"What do you do when you aren't here?" All of us have pondered that, but never receive a straight answer. This time was no exception.

"Oh, I wear a lot of different hats, or in my case, noses. I never have a dull moment."

"You're a bit of a mystery, you know."

Derek laughed and put an arm around my shoulder.

"You're not going to tell me, are you?"

"Don't you keep some layers of yourself hidden?"

I couldn't argue with that. He knows nothing about Kendra, or my past relationship. Derek said, "I like being known as Minno. If I get too much into the other facets of my life, it would chip away at who Minno is. Do you understand?"

I supposed I did a little bit. We all keep bits and pieces of ourselves tucked deeply away so no one else could see them.

"Can I ask you something else?"

"What is that now?"

"Can I give you a hug?"

It was like the air around Derek's head lit up, like an aura. There was something so mystical about him, but powerful and loving all the same. He came right over and wrapped his arms around me. For some reason I didn't understand at that moment, I began to cry. It was like all of the emotions from the previous days flooded out of me like a water main break. Even though he didn't say anything, I believed Derek knew and felt my pain and need to be loved. I literally buried my head in his chest, and he just gently held me. I couldn't explain it, but it was almost like God was holding me Himself.

After what seemed like a half hour passed, I stepped back and looked at Derek. The self-doubt popped up like a prairie dog out of the sand, and I immediately looked away. Derek turned my chin toward him and said, "It's okay. You needed to let it all out."

"Maybe you should carry around tissue boxes along with your red noses since we women keep crying on your shoulders."

Derek laughed and kissed my forehead. "I will definitely take that into consideration. All right, my friend. You have a good shift today, and I will see you next weekend. Are you doing anything special this week?"

"I have a few things planned with my parents and my best friend."

"Awesome. You have fun, and remember you are loved."

Derek walked back in the direction of the motel while I remained on the pier. I couldn't believe how my life had changed in the past few months. New career, new friends. My parents recently told me that they were both really happy for me that I found Serenity Savor. I believe it found me. I hadn't realized how much I needed something new in my life. My landlord Paul was right—I needed to rebuild. With this new information about the finances at the motel, I was confused about what else I could add. Remembering Derek's words, I walked to the end of the pier, looked towards the mountains, and prayed.

"Heavenly Father, I want to give thanks for my job at Serenity Savor and for all of the wonderful people who work there. I want to help, Lord, but I don't really know what else I could do. Honestly, I feel like a failure. Five years of college down the drain. My marriage down the drain. I want to believe my life has purpose, but I don't know what that is. Please help me see what I can do because Renee and her family deserve so much good to happen to them. Thank you so much for sending Derek into my life, though he is a bit mysterious. In a good way, of course. And,

Lord…please help Kendra. I am so scared about what happened to her last night, and even now. I pray you hear me, Lord."

With that, one of the cruise ship's steam whistles sounded, and I nearly fell off the pier because I wasn't expecting it. I laughed and said, "Well, God, you obviously heard me."

Chapter 14

I walked into the lobby feeling very hopeful. I had even treated myself to a new outfit. I was thinking about what Derek told me regarding the woman who used to work there. I thought if I presented a more professional image it would help. I also made an appointment for next week with my hairdresser who has her own salon, but also works out of her home as well. She usually sees me in her home to help keep the cost down for me. I am very blessed with the friends that I have. I am planning for a new color as part of my rebuilding process.

"Hi, Heather!"

"Hey." she said in a monotone voice.

"Everything okay?"

Heather looked at me with a fierce expression. "Well, thanks to you not checking to make sure the coffee pot was turned on last night with the timer, we had a lot of unhappy guests this morning, which is actually an understatement!"

My heart started thumping. "Heather, I checked it last night. I know I did."

"Well, obviously you didn't check hard enough! It was a nightmare this morning! You really need to be more careful!"

Something short-circuited within me at that moment. "You know what, Heather? I get to yell at myself, but nobody else has that permission!"

At that point, Renee stepped out of the house. "What is going on out here? I can hear both of you all the way in the kitchen."

Before Heather could say anything, I immediately shot my mouth off. I was still reeling from the whole situation with Kendra and I had it with people losing it on me.

"I made a mistake, which obviously is not allowed here. You both knew when you hired me that this was all new to me. I am tired of always coming up short with everyone!"

I could feel the tears coming, but I didn't care. I was done.

"I'm sorry I'm not perfect! Take a number with everyone else who thinks I am a piece of shit!"

With that, I grabbed my purse and fled out the door. I can't believe all that I said, but my emotions were at volcano level. I know they are all dealing with crap, but so am I. I don't throw it all around on everyone like a hose. I went straight to my apartment and slammed the door. I flopped down in my recliner and lost it. I am so sick of everything caving in on me.

About a half hour later, I heard a knock on my door. I didn't want to answer. Then, I heard a soft voice call out my name. It was Renee. I figured I was getting fired, so why postpone the inevitable? I dragged myself to the front door and opened it. I was shocked at first because Renee's eyes were all red. I could tell she had been crying.

"Hey. Can I please come in and talk with you?"

"I already know I am being fired, so why drag it out?"

"You're not being fired. Please, let's talk."

I let Renee come in and offered her a soft drink.

"You got anything stronger?" She asked. She wasn't joking either.

"I have a sweet wine from that cute winery in town."

"Perfect!"

I got out the bottle and poured two glasses. Renee was sitting on my couch looking like she was about to collapse. I suddenly had a flash go through my mind.

"Who's watching the desk?"

"Oh, my dear daughter is. She happens to have the night off from the bar, and after the way she treated you, she is staying there until I go back."

I sat on the opposite side of Renee. She drained half of the wine that was in the glass. I could relate.

"I normally don't drink like this, but I am at the point of "who cares" right now."

"Renee, what is going on? That wasn't like Heather to act like that, though it wasn't right. I made a mistake, which I don't remember doing anyway."

"It wasn't right of her to go off on you, and I am not trying to make excuses for her. Unfortunately, she wasn't in a good frame of mind, and it was more than just the coffee."

I had a strong feeling Renee was about to share with me the situation Derek filled me in on earlier. I had to act like I was clueless because I would never want to get him in trouble. He has been a lifeline for all of us. Renee set down her glass and leaned forward.

"There is something going on that you are not aware of."

I remained silent. Renee's hands shook a little.

"Serenity Savor is in jeopardy of closing."

Renee began to sob again. This was actually worse than what Derek shared.

"Renee, what happened? I don't understand."

She took a couple of minutes to get herself together. I gave her the time to compose herself. I could tell how difficult this was for her.

"When I was a little girl, my parents ran a motel. We were living in Florida at the time. I helped my mom with everything, and I was hooked. The guests loved me and always brought me toys and snacks and stuff. She loved what she did. My dad mainly did maintenance and the books. He was a numbers guy and loved working outside. He spoke with the guests, but my mom was the people person."

I could tell this would not have a happy ending.

"When I was a teenager, I was actually being groomed to take over the motel. I was so excited. Then the unthinkable happened. That was the year when a major hurricane hit the state. Unfortunately, the storm wiped our place out."

I sucked in my breath.

"My parents' motel was a very popular spot. That hurricane, though, changed everything."

I remained silent.

"My family and all of our guests had to seek shelter at an evacuation center. I was never so scared in my entire life. When it was over and we were allowed to go back...I will never forget the looks on my parents' faces. Our motel and home were blown to bits. The devastation was beyond anything we could comprehend."

Renee sat back on the couch and wiped her eyes.

"Something changed within my dad. My mom wanted to rebuild, but my dad wanted no part of it. He became a shell of who he was and even got into alcoholism. You probably think it's ironic as I am drinking all of this wine."

"Not everybody who drinks is an alcoholic." I said, knowingly.

"One morning my mom and I woke up and my dad was gone. We found an envelope on the kitchen counter where we were staying and it basically said he couldn't deal with what had happened and that we were better off without him."

Tears welled up in my eyes at that point. I would have never guessed. You truly never know what a person has endured throughout their life, do you?

"That's why I mentioned to you in our first meeting that I understood more than you knew. We never saw or heard from my dad again. I don't even know if he is still alive. My mom died a few years later. They say people can die of a broken heart, and I believe that is exactly what happened to her. She lost her husband and the place that meant so much to her. There I was—an orphan in my early twenties."

I put a hand on her arm.

"I had no siblings, so I was truly alone. The only work I knew was the motel. I had insurance money left to me, so I knew one day I would open up my own place. I felt I needed to keep the legacy going. I wanted a change of location, though. A good friend back then invited me to go skiing with her in the Adirondacks. I knew

I needed to get away and regroup, so I went with her. Well, it was love at first sight. I loved the mountains and upstate New York. I was only a beginner skier, but I loved the lodge we stayed at. Before we left, I saw that they were looking for a front desk guest relations manager. I wasn't even looking for a job at that time, but I opened my mouth anyway. Well, I was hired that day. The lodge owner at the time knew about the hurricane, so when I told him what happened he offered to cover relocation expenses. I told him it wasn't necessary, but he insisted. So, three weeks later I officially left the south to a life in the mountains, and I never looked back. I fell in love with the ski lodge and worked there for almost ten years. I even became an advanced skier!"

I smiled along with Renee.

"And you will never guess who my instructor was."

"Oh my gosh! Keith?"

Renee nodded with a twinkle in her eyes. "I thought he was the best-looking guy in the world, and could he ski! He is actually the manager of the slopes now. We started dating immediately, and he wound up proposing to me on Christmas Day on the chair lift!"

"That's amazing!"

"Heather came almost two years later, but we loved working at the lodge together. It was a brand new life. Not that anyone could make up for the loss of my parents, but he opened up my heart to new possibilities. I still never gave up on my dream of opening up another motel."

I leaned back. I was so moved by her story.

"One day Keith and I took a drive when Heather was in school. We came to this cute town called Lake George about an hour away and came across a motel with a sign that said 'For Sale.' I am a very spiritual person, and I just felt that motel calling me. Keith knew about my dream, so he asked if I wanted to inquire about it. We called the number on the sign, and that day we found Serenity Savor."

Renee took another sip of wine. "The lady who owned it was ready to retire, and none of her children wanted to take it over. She kept it immaculate. I just knew it was mine. We prayed about it that night and the next day we made arrangements to transfer ownership. I kept my job at the lodge until they found a new person to take over and was fully trained. I knew I would miss the lodge, but it was time for the next step. By the way, my replacement is still there, and she is very happy."

"Oh wow! That's terrific!"

"I took over her motel and gave it a new name—Serenity Savor. This town is full of serenity, and it is something to be savored."

"I think it's a wonderful name."

Renee looked at her watch. "Are you hungry?"

I actually was. I was planning on ordering something to be delivered at the motel tonight until the brown stuff hit the fan.

"Before I tell you the rest, let's get something to eat. My treat."

"Are you sure?"

Renee laughed. "I'm not destitute yet. Besides, we both have to eat."

Chapter 15

"Oh my gosh! This burger is the best!"

Renee was cracking me up. She was *really* enjoying her cheeseburger she ordered at a popular local BBQ joint. She reminded me of my mother with her loading the burger with all kinds of toppings. I always used to joke with my mom to have some meat with those toppings. Renee's face was lathered with mayonnaise, pieces of onion, and other remnants. I didn't judge; she was in pain and she deserved to indulge a little.

"What?" she asked, grinning.

"You have half of your burger all over your face." I grinned.

Renee shrugged her shoulders and wiped her face off with her napkin. "I usually don't eat like this. Keith is very big into health and fitness, so when I cook, our meals are very balanced and health-focused. I love a lot of what we have, but when you are facing a monumental crisis, somehow a Brussel sprout doesn't quite do the trick."

She must have seen my mouth and eyes scrunch up because she pointed a French fry at me and stated, "Don't knock Brussel sprouts. They're not that bad if they're cooked right."

"You're quite convincing with that French fry pointing directly at me." I joked. I am beginning to believe that French fries have it in for me at restaurants.

Renee sat back and looked at me pointedly. I wasn't sure what was going through her mind at that moment.

"You are really easy to be around. You have a calming effect when people talk with you. Heather even said it."

I nearly spit out my soda. I asked incredulously, "Heather?"

Renee held up her hands. "I know, it's hard to believe after what happened earlier. But, it's true. Heather is a true Type A, and she doesn't mince words. Deep down, though, she has a huge heart. She admires the way you care so much about people and your work."

Renee's expression became very serious. I had a feeling Part 2 of Serenity Savor's fate was coming.

"When the motel first opened, it was very popular because it was new. Keith, Heather, and I worked tirelessly those first couple of years. I was in my element. This was what I was born to do, and I didn't care how many hours or sleepless nights I had to endure. I felt like my mother was with me every step of the way. Keith continued to work at the lodge, but in the summer months he had more time to devote to the motel, especially the pool maintenance. It was great because I close after Halloween and don't open until April, which is Keith's busiest time at the slopes. We thought we had it all."

Renee took a long sip of her water.

"The problem with having it all is you get stuck in a comfort zone and take it for granted that business is always going to be wonderful, and nothing further has to be done because guests love you and will always come back. I fell into the trap of believing I didn't have to do anything different because I had the best motel in Lake George."

Renee snickered and shook her head.

"After five years of running Serenity Savor changes in the economy began happening, but I wasn't worried. Adirondack Lodge was doing really well, but of course it remains open all year. I began to notice subtle changes with our numbers. It wasn't a big deal until almost a decade went by. I said something about it to Keith and he examined the books. My loving husband suggested that I speak with other hotel and motel owners about their numbers and possible ideas, but I did not take it to heart. Truth was, I felt insulted. Heather even suggested I stay open all year, but I wanted a break in the winter. It was what my parents always did. Our family goes away every November for Thanksgiving, and then Keith and I usually sneak away around Valentine's Day. I have never had a summer vacation, but it never bothered me. Well, last year I decided to hire another desk clerk because I needed more time to attend to other administrative matters. She was in her fifties and had excellent credentials and experience. She was a manager at a major department store for many years, plus she had her own online business like E-bay or something like that. I figured I hit the jackpot."

The server came over and asked if we needed anything else. We both were full from our meals, but decided on coffee. Renee did not seem anxious at all to leave. If Heather was in a mood earlier, she must be seething by now.

"Roxanne, the desk clerk, was amazing with her speed and efficiency. She could check people in and out in a flash. She kept the office and desk neat as a pin and constantly arranged everything. She was a bit OCD. It wasn't until three months into her being employed with us that I started reading bad reviews about her on the travel websites."

"Uh oh."

"Yup. And people read that stuff and treat it as gospel, let me tell you. For one thing, she apparently was not friendly to guests, especially when they came in with questions. Her response was something akin to "that's why we have brochures so you don't have to ask where things are."

"Oh jeez."

"Wait, it gets better. One time a guest came in, picked up a particular brochure, but had the audacity to not put it back with the others. Roxanne called this poor woman out and stated that since she had worked so hard on arranging the brochures, the least she could do was put it back in its correct location."

"Holy crap!"

Renee swallowed what she had been drinking and nodded her head. "I was mortified. So of course I was faced with the lovely task of having to confront Roxanne with all of this. I even printed everything out to show her I wasn't making any of this up. She wasn't really that apologetic, but stated she would try to be more "people-friendly." Well, that lasted about a week. After personally being approached about another incident to do with Roxanne, I had no choice but to let her go. It was right around August, but I didn't care. I didn't want any more bad publicity for Serenity Savor. Unfortunately, the damage was done."

"I'm shocked you would take a chance with someone else again after all that mess."

"Well, I felt I had to because Heather was offered the night bar manager position at the Paddlewheel, and it meant more money and experience for her. You know she wants to work in a big city hotel someday. As a mother, I couldn't take that away from her. Plus, she would kill me if she knew I shared this, but I feel very comfortable with you—Heather offered to work for me without getting paid to help me save money."

I had to put on my best Oscar performance because Derek already filled me in on this information, but the way Renee disclosed it brought genuine tears to my eyes. This woman has been through so much, and yet is not filled with any anger or self-pity. I don't know how she does it.

"My numbers are really horrible from last season. Last night I woke up in the middle of the night with a horrible nightmare and panic attack. I don't have a lot of reservations for after Memorial Weekend. The majority of phone calls have been for general information. I told Heather around three in the morning that if we have one more bad season, I may have no other option but to close the motel. It's bringing back all of my childhood trauma with what my parents went through."

Renee's eyes filled with tears too. I felt sick for her.

"That was why Heather was in such a foul mood when you came in. She barely got enough sleep, and then the issue happened with the coffee. I am not blaming you; it was an honest mistake. I am just trying to paint the whole picture of why she lost it on you."

She's not getting paid either, I thought, but I didn't say anything. I felt even more terrible that I messed up this morning. Renee looked really exhausted.

"I am praying for a miracle. The only other person I have shared this with is Derek, but we have such a long history with him. I have stretched my family to the max. I really don't have many other options. We don't want to take out a loan and risk going into further debt."

I leaned forward and looked her directly in the eyes. With more conviction than I actually felt, I said, "Renee, I really believe things will work out. You are too wonderful a person to have your dreams ripped away from you like this. I don't know the answer, but I do believe something will work out."

Renee put a hand on my arm. "I really appreciate that, Sage, but I admit I am losing hope. Keith and I have discussed the possibility of selling the motel after this season and buying a small cabin near the lodge. I could always get another job at Adirondack. I always loved it there anyway."

I think Renee was trying to convince us both, but I could see the deep pain in her eyes. Her true passion was running Serenity Savor.

"Renee, you told me when we first met that you wanted to open a bed and breakfast. I don't believe God wants you to give up on that. You're too special and creative."

"Then tell me what I should do, Sage, because I am out of answers!"

A few people looked over at us because her comment was stated loudly. Renee apologized and stated it was time for her to go back to the motel and relieve Heather. Before she left, Renee stated, "Sage, if you have any ideas, I am open to anything. But as of now, this is my last season."

Chapter 16

"I can't believe all of this." said Gia, shaking her head.

I was at Gia's condo the following evening. I had texted her the next morning and told her I really needed a friend. She immediately called and offered for me to come over that evening for dinner and even stay overnight. I decided to stay because I needed a change of scenery. Gia works until four, so I arrived around six to give her time to change, relax, and prepare for my coming over. Her condo has two bedrooms and is a nice size. Evan is living at his parents' house helping to take care of his mother who has a serious debilitating condition. Gia confided in me one time that she believes that is part of why he hasn't proposed yet; his first obligation is to his family. He has a younger brother, but he lives in another state on the West Coast. Gia has been really understanding, but she admitted it worries her at times because he tries to be Superman. Evan's father suffers with depression, so Evan is the main caretaker. From working at nursing homes, Gia often sees family members who still beat themselves up with massive guilt that they had to put their loved ones in an advanced level care facility. She is a strong believer that at times it is more loving and honorable to make that choice because there are more resources available to their loved ones than there is in a regular home setting. Gia has shared her views with Evan, who does not agree. Gia tries to support him as best as she can, but she prays he will be more open-minded.

Gia had a couple of pizzas delivered for our dinner. As we were munching on our slices, I shared with her everything that I learned from Renee about the status of Serenity Savor. Gia could not believe what she was hearing.

"Gia, I am so sick of everything in my life falling apart. Here I thought I was starting over in a positive direction, and another earthquake hits again."

I really felt like giving up, but I didn't share that with Gia. As a healthcare worker, she has to take statements like that seriously, plus she is my best friend. Inwardly, I felt like I was dying.

"I love this family so much. They are so resilient and supportive of each other. I wish I could help them, but I don't know what to do. I can't give up my pay because I need to live too."

Gia was quiet for a few moments, and then suddenly sat straight up on the couch.

"Sage, didn't you mention that part of the issue was that Renee didn't advertise or something like that?"

I swallowed my iced tea and stated, "Renee admitted that she got too comfortable with doing well and word-of-mouth referrals, so she didn't really market or anything. Now she feels it is biting herself in the butt, so to say. Plus, she had major issues with that other desk clerk."

"Sage, you are really good at marketing."

I stared at her, dumbfounded.

"I've never done marketing in my life."

Gia practically burst, she was so excited. I thought she was going to spontaneously combust.

"Your teaching!"

"What are you talking about? There was no marketing involved in that."

"Of course there was! Think about it, what do you do in a lesson plan?"

I rubbed my forehead out of frustration. I loved Gia, but sometimes she ran a marathon to get to her point.

"Gia no offense, but I have a huge headache to begin with, and I came here to de-stress, not the other way around. Please explain what you mean."

Gia finished her mushroom slice of pizza and grabbed a notebook and pen.

"It's really not that different than what I do at the nursing homes. I have to adapt all of my activities to accommodate all of my patients. The big difference is I only deal with the creative arts. You, as an in-class support teacher, have to deal with a variety of subjects."

This was true.

"Sage, I never told you this, but I was blown away when you came up with the Explorers rap song to reach your students."

As much as I appreciated her praise, it was painful as well. I did that project before I became ill, and the kids absolutely loved it. Other teachers wanted to use the idea, or modify it for another purpose. Still, I didn't see how this related to Serenity Savor.

Gia continued, "Do you remember telling me that you were so upset that the students in your group were struggling to understand and even care about history? You wished you could teach it in a way that the kids could relate to it? Then, bam! You woke up in the middle of the night and were inspired to write the rap song because you were studying about Christopher Columbus and other explorers. When you start a lesson plan or, in my case, an activity plan, you identify what your main objectives are."

I started to see a light into where she was going.

"Your objective was to make history fun and educational for them so it would make sense and accommodate their levels and abilities. It was brilliant because music is something that is universal no matter where your cognitive level is at. When you market a product or service, you look at what will be best for your client instead of a cookie-cutter approach, then you utilize the resources you have to help achieve that goal."

Gia's brain was working overtime tonight. She should start her own consulting practice. I was hooked on what she was saying. I never thought the skills I learned to become a teacher would come into play again in a totally different setting. Gia picked up the pen and started jotting down notes.

"Come on, girlfriend." Gia said enthusiastically, handing me a pen. "Let's form a plan to save Serenity Savor."

We worked for over two hours, and then Gia had to turn in because she had to work the next morning. I won't be on shift again until Friday evening. I told Gia I am supposed to get more hours the closer it gets to Memorial Weekend, but I was really getting worried. My savings account was dwindling, so this job was a timely and welcomed blessing; now it's in jeopardy. My parents keep telling me I can always move back home if I wanted to, but the truth was, giving up my apartment would just feel like another casualty from the past year. Plus, there was the issue of Kendra. They still don't know that she called me the other day. The weird thing is I noticed a missed call earlier from an unknown number. It wasn't the original number Kendra provided, but the exchange was the same. There was no voicemail, and I didn't call it back. I could not have handled another verbal run-in with that asshole Glen. I still keep replaying the slapping sounds in my head. I laid my head on a very fluffy pillow and drifted off to sleep.

I woke up early the next morning and joined Gia for breakfast before she left for work. She cooked amazing French toast and used maple syrup from Vermont. Gia and her sister go to the Vermont Country Store every year and stock up on syrup. Someday, I will join them. I became very reclusive the past couple of years and I plan on changing that.

"Gia, have you ever skied?"

Gia laughed and stated, "Well, that's a random out-of-the-blue question."

"Renee's husband is a ski instructor at Adirondack Lodge. He's also a manager there. I tried skiing in my youth group days, but I hurt my back."

"That's right. Someone left a pair of skis on the slope, and you tumbled over them."

"Yup. Hundreds of people on the slope, and I am the one who had the misfortune of meeting up with the rogue skis. It was a shame because I was really getting good on the bunny slope."

Gia washed her dishes. "Are you thinking of trying it again?"

"I don't know, maybe. I can't think about much more except the future of the motel."

"I never had a desire to try it. I don't know. I know it sounds crazy because we live in the mountains, but not everyone who lives by the ocean enjoys going to the beach."

"This is true. Speaking of the beach, my parents are planning a trip to the Jersey Shore in June. They want to go to Atlantic City and Wildwood."

"Good for them. Are you going with them?"

I swallowed my orange juice and shook my head.

"I can't because of the new job. It's okay. I will join them at another time."

Gia began gathering up her purse and keys. I have a spare key to her condo because I have house-sat for her in the past. Gia told me I could hang out as long as I needed to.

"Are you going to talk with Renee today?"

"I am going to call her and ask if we can meet tomorrow. I am going to work on putting all of this together in a more organized fashion. I also want to clean my apartment today."

"Well, if you need anything else, just text or call. It was great having company last night. Evan has been spending a lot of time at home. I understand he is putting his family first, which is the right thing, but I feel like I have been excluded. I have told him before that I will not be treated like a side dish."

"Have you sat down and discussed this with him?"

"Not yet, but I'm getting close. I want to take my vacation over Fourth of July, but at this point, I may postpone."

Evan and Gia love the Fourth of July. They travel to a different area every year to see a massive fireworks display. Last year they went to Boston. I have a feeling if Evan doesn't do something soon to reassure Gia, there will be a fireworks event quite a far cry from the ones in the sky.

"I am sure Evan will reach out. He's probably just feeling overwhelmed."

"When you are committed to someone, you still make them a priority. I am very sorry his parents have so many issues, but if he thinks he can fix everything by himself and ignore the other people in his life, hence me, then there is a real problem."

I have never seen Gia this upset and disillusioned before. She is usually so positive. *Maybe there is more than she is telling me?* I wondered. Gia waved and didn't say anymore. When she closed the door, I walked over to her Bay Window. She had a magnificent view of Prospect Mountain, an exquisite natural elevation with a lot of history attached to it. Locals and tourists can either take a drive up to a certain spot and ride a tram car the rest of the way to the summit, or for the more fit and healthy, actually hike the trail. Maybe someday I will be able to do the latter.

My cell phone rang, and it was from Serenity Savor. I felt my heart start to thump. I picked it up.

"Hello?"

"Hi Sage, it's Heather."

I was shocked to hear her voice, even more because she was calm. I figured after her having to cover my three hours on one of her nights off that she would be creating a voodoo doll out of me and sticking pins in it.

"Hi. Is everything okay?"

"I just wanted to apologize for being such a bitch to you yesterday. You certainly did not deserve it, especially since we discovered the real reason the coffee pot didn't turn on."

"Oh yeah?" I was interested in this piece of news.

"The timer was old and apparently conked out that night. You did everything right. It was a faulty gadget."

The good thing about cell phones and other mobile devices is that you can perform other activities while holding them in one hand or, in my case, putting it on speaker. I set the phone down as she was apologizing, and I was jumping up and down mouthing *'I told you so! I told you so!'* Then I did a little happy dance. Yes, it was a bit juvenile, but it is not often I am on the receiving end of amends.

"Are you still there, Sage?"

I brought myself back to adult reality and picked up the phone. "Yes, Heather, I am. Sorry, I was trying to shoo away a fly." Not the truth, but it sounded good.

"Anyway, I wanted to reach out because it was totally wrong of me to lose it on you like that. I know Mom filled you in on what's been going on. Things aren't exactly peachy around here."

Talk about an understatement. *No, it's more like rotten apples*, I responded mentally.

"I feel so bad for all of you. I wish I could do more." I answered. Hopefully I can.

"Well, just try to hang in there with us. We really want you here and don't want to lose you."

Heather sounded really humble and sincere and for a moment I felt a tad guilty for my childish act before. Nah, I still felt justified.

"Will you be coming back next week?" Heather got right to the point.

"Yes. Yes, I am. In fact, I want to talk with your Mom. Is she available today?"

"Not today. She and Dad took a day trip today just to get away. I think they were heading to Ausable Chasm or High Falls Gorge. She will be around tomorrow, though."

"Okay, good. I will stop by tomorrow."

Heather was silent for a moment. "You aren't leaving, are you?" She sounded really worried.

"No, I promise. Just some ideas I wanted to discuss."

"Alright. I will let her know you will be coming by tomorrow. Thanks for understanding, Sage."

I know it wasn't easy for her to make that call. I have a new respect for Heather, especially with the knowledge of her working at the motel without a salary. If what Gia and I discussed and put together last night actually works all of them will have a powerful cash flow again, God willing.

Chapter 17

The next day was warm and sunny. The sky was a brilliant blue with hardly any clouds visible. Tourism was beginning to come alive again in Lake George. Paul called me last night and informed me a new family was moving in the little house next door sometime the following week. He said they are fantastic people and believes I will get along with them really well, which is great because I am feeling ready to start socializing again. Heather also sent me a text inviting me to hang out at the Paddlewheel and hear a band on a night she was working sometime. The same text had also requested me to meet up with her Mom at ten the next morning. I was on my way to Serenity Savor now.

As I started up the walkway towards the motel, I noticed a couple staring at the building. The man was over 6 foot, and the woman with him was shorter. I could tell the man was into sports and his female companion dressed very hip and stylish. I walked up to them and said hello.

"Do you work here?" the man asked excitedly.

"Yes, but not today. I am just meeting with my boss. Please come in, though."

"Great! Thank you. We will."

The man and woman followed me in. Renee and Heather were both at the desk. I told them that this couple were interested in the motel.

"This is lovely!" the man exclaimed. The woman with him agreed and smiled.

"Well, thank you very much." said Renee, practically blushing. When she didn't say anything else, I took the lead.

"What are your names?" I asked.

"My name is Nikki, and my husband's name is Kevin. We actually live near the Jersey Shore, but thought we would check out this place called Lake George. One of Kevin's coworkers told him about it."

"Where about in Jersey?" I asked.

They mentioned a town that was in between two major boardwalks, which were Seaside Heights and Point Pleasant.

"Oh wow, that's awesome! My grandmother used to go with us all the time to Seaside when we took trips to the Shore. We also went to Point Pleasant. She rode amusements with us all the time." I shared.

"That's great!" Kevin stated enthusiastically. I really liked this couple.

"Do you want to make a reservation?" Heather got right to the point again. I grinned to myself.

"I don't know," Nikki started. "We had some time off, so we decided to come up here and check everything out. It's beautiful here."

I began by saying, "Well, I just started at the motel this year, but I can tell you that you are not going to find a better place to stay than Serenity Savor. Best staff, friendly, and very clean!"

Renee finally chimed in. "Oh, you have no idea what kind of questions I get regarding cleanliness here. One woman actually came right out and asked me if patrons don't get clean sheets just because we're a motel! I really wanted to say to her that all of the rooms were clean except for hers."

Nikki and Kevin doubled over laughing. Heather even laughed. We all needed it with the current drama and crisis going on.

"Well, what do you think, hon?" Kevin asked his wife. "I don't think you're going to find better people than them."

"Why not? We'll stay for one night and then decide tomorrow what to do."

Heather took over with checking them in, but I could tell she was pleased. It's not always easy to book people during the week, especially in the off-season. This was a bonus for them. Plus, Nikki and Kevin added a mammoth amount of energy that was contagious. I told my new friends I had a meeting, but that I would hopefully see them again.

"Why don't you hang out with us when you're done?" Kevin offered, and Nikki agreed.

I was caught off-guard. I mean, I just met them, but they seemed like awesome people. I was about to say no, but it was almost like an invisible spirit tapped me on the shoulder and wagged its finger at me. I realized that I needed to move forward in many ways, just as I was about to encourage Renee to do the same.

"Sure. I'm not sure how long we will be meeting for, though. I don't want to hold you up."

"Don't worry, we will be around until you're done. We have to unpack anyway. Take your time."

I waved goodbye, and then Renee and I stepped inside the house. Mocha greeted me right away. After I let her lay on my red leather jacket back in February, I assume I made the cut with her acceptance of me in her territory. When I walked into the dining room, I was shocked at the spread of food on the table.

"Wow!"

"I actually baked a lot of it. Baking and cooking always relaxes me."

I eagerly grabbed a cinnamon bun and applied the melted cream cheese topping. I thought I died and went to food heaven.

"O M G. You should make these available at the continental breakfast!"

"If I had enough guests staying, I probably would." Renee stated with a hint of disillusionment in her tone. This was a fantastic way of segueing into my plan. As if she read my mind, Renee looked at my folder I brought with me.

"So what did you want to talk about with me? Heather gave me the impression it was important."

"It is. Before I begin, can I have some coffee first?"

"Of course. I will get some for us. Please help yourself to anything on the table. It's a good thing Keith is at the lodge today. He would be scolding me for all of this."

I knew she was kidding, but I was also hoping this situation wasn't affecting their marriage.

"Heather mentioned that you and Keith took a day off and went to Ausable Chasm or High Falls Gorge. Did you have a good time? You both needed it."

Renee peeked around the corner, as if she was checking to see if anyone else was overhearing our conversation. She gestured for me to follow her in the kitchen. A little alarm bell sounded in my head. I followed her into the kitchen where the smell of hazelnut coffee was brewing.

"Smells good." I said, trying to lighten the mood.

"Thanks. I wanted to make sure that Heather can't overhear what I am about to tell you. We told Heather a cover story yesterday. We wanted her to think we went on a day trip, but the truth is…we were looking at cabins to move to."

I felt like a hot poker stabbed me in the heart. My breath became a little shallow. Renee was really sinking into defeat. She was about to give up.

"After our conversation the other day, I spoke with my husband and we figured it was time to suck it up and accept the reality about where things stand with this place. Keith is stressed to the max and he hates seeing what this is doing to me. He is also worried about Heather. This can't be all about me and my dreams. I've had a good run. Yeah, I would have loved to make this motel or even another one into a bed-and-breakfast, but some dreams just aren't meant to come alive. I already have been offered a head culinary position at Adirondack after October. It's not all bad, Sage. I feel terrible for you because you just started here, but I am sure Keith could help you find another job at the lodge or somewhere else."

Renee brought our two cups of coffee over to the table.

"In time, we will tell Heather. But for now she needs to focus on her job at the Paddlewheel and preparing for school. Thank God I earmarked some of the insurance money for her education so I didn't ruin another dream."

"Okay, Renee, this is the perfect time to get into what I was about to discuss. First of all, it sounds like you have already decided your future without even looking at other options. That's why I am here this morning. I have some ideas that may help get you to where you want to be."

"I don't have to decide my future. Look at what happened to my parents. We just aren't meant to move forward in this industry."

"Renee, that was due to a massive hurricane. Unfortunately, we can't predict Mother Nature. A lot of people were devastated by that hurricane, I am sure. In this situation, you can make some other choices. It's just a matter of how much you want to leave your comfort zone."

"You sound like a shrink." Renee said with little affect.

"I see a shrink, so that is probably why I sound like one." Plus, I had Paul, my pseudo-shrink.

Renee became a little more animated. "You do?"

"Yep. She is located in Saratoga. Been going there for about six months now."

Renee picked at her blueberry muffin. "Is she taking new patients?"

"I believe she is. She's wonderful. I can give you her name and number before I leave today, if you like."

Renee suddenly looked very sad and pensive. This news obviously touched a nerve within her.

"I see her only once a month due to budget issues, but what I get out of her one hour is worth four sessions. I will be seeing her soon because I have a lot to discuss with her." *Particularly about Kendra,* I thought to myself.

Renee pushed hair out of her eyes. She looked very tired and drained. I took the papers out of my folder and placed them between us.

"Renee, this could be what makes the difference with Serenity Savor moving forward or not. Just please listen to what I am about to share."

Chapter 18

"So, how does this work?" Renee asked.

She was sitting on a dark green plush couch inside the office of Erika Moseley, a licensed individual and family counselor in the town of Saratoga. She was a striking African-American woman who dressed impeccably, but was so down to earth she immediately exuded warmth and compassion. Renee instantly liked her.

"You just tell me whatever is on your mind." Erika said, encouragingly.

"We might be here all afternoon..." Renee said with a smirk.

"Don't worry about the time. If you notice, I have no clock in here. I never want my guests to feel like they have to watch the clock when they are in the middle of pouring their hearts out. That's why I schedule everyone two hours apart. It's worked for me so far."

"I noticed you used the word guest."

Erika laughed. "I knew you would pick up on that being you work in the hospitality industry. I never liked the words patient or client. They're too...clinical. When you come in my office, you are my guest. You're trusting me with your deepest thoughts and feelings, and I will do everything I can to make you feel welcome.

After all, you could have gone somewhere else but you chose to come here. That is worth me going out of my way for you."

Renee shook her head. "No wonder Sage raved about you so much."

"The feeling was very mutual, believe me. Now, you gave a little insight into what brought you in here today on your intake form, but I want to hear it from you. Take your time."

Renee clasped her hands together. Deep down she always knew she needed to see a therapist since the trauma with her family but never actually followed through on it. Renee was thrown into the position of having to take care of herself and totally uproot her life. When she began her job at Adirondack Lodge and fell in love with Keith she thought that would suffice in burying her deep-seeded emotions towards all of the loss in her past. She explained everything in depth to Erika, including biting details about staying in the shelter not knowing what was happening to her home and later finding remnants of their belongings all over their property after the hurricane. She particularly honed in on a ceramic vase she made for her mother the year before in an art class, and her mother treasured it. Now it was nothing but broken shards of glass on top of dirty and cracked pavement.

"I was thinking about that vase the other day. It's like a metaphor for what life feels like. You work so hard at something, and bam! It's ripped away from you just like that."

Erika nodded empathically. She didn't say anything until she was sure Renee was done sharing. When Renee remained silent, Erika leaned forward and stated quietly, "And now you feel like you're reliving what happened in Florida all over again."

Tears flooded Renee's eyes as she nodded. "I didn't want to think about it anymore. I thought I had buried it all. I found a new life here, I loved my job, my husband, and my daughter. There was no reason to bring up all that horror. We bought the motel in Lake George and I was doing really well, but now...."

Renee started to cry. She hadn't cried in years; now, she was sobbing all of the time. She wondered if she was losing her mind. As if Erika could read her mind, she said, "There is nothing wrong with crying your eyes out. I have a lot of stock in Kleenex."

Renee actually smiled amongst the tears. With that, she grabbed a few tissues and blew her nose.

"Hey, these are nicer tissues than mine. Want to trade?"

Erika laughed really loud. "Now see, you were able to make a joke while you were so tearful there. There is always hope."

Renee composed herself and took a few sips of water from the cup Erika offered her in the beginning of their session. She took notice of a Keurig machine next to Erika's desk.

"You want some coffee, my dear?"

"Wow, you do notice everything. Sure, if that's okay."

"Of course it is. Why don't you go up and choose a flavor?"

Renee did as she was instructed and picked out a chocolate donut-flavored coffee. Since she was spilling her guts, she might as well go for the jugular with coffee. Erika would not let her make her own coffee, though. Renee went to protest, but Erika stated again that Renee was her guest and should be treated as such. Renee had a flashback to her own mother. It was exactly the same thing her mother would have done.

"You remind me so much of my own mother. She would have loved you."

"I live by the Golden Rule, my love."

"I had a totally different idea of what this would be like."

Erika handed Renee her coffee. Then she made a cup for herself. Renee was starting to feel really relaxed and comfortable.

"You mean you expected to come in here, lay on the couch, and have me ask you tough questions?"

Renee smiled. "I don't know. I was expecting more of…maybe, being judged."

"Nope, no courtroom here. Seriously, I know what you mean, and I saw some of that when I was in graduate school. People go into this line of work for many different reasons, but I truly wanted to help empower those in my path. People come in here already scarred; they don't need to come into some therapist's office and be bullied and beaten up emotionally."

Renee filled Erika in the current status of Serenity Savor and what Sage and her friend proposed. Erika thought the ideas were wonderful, but she sensed resistance on Renee's part.

"So what are you afraid of?"

Renee looked down at her shoes. She knew, but didn't want to voice it out loud.

"Renee, let me ask you something. If you were standing in front of a brick wall, or any wall for that matter, and you were smashing your hand against it multiple times, wouldn't you get a bad bruise on your hand?"

Renee wasn't sure what that had to do with anything, but she agreed.

"Well, that's what trauma does to a person's brain. Every time an intense incident occurs, it's like your brain is being smashed against that wall. Eventually a big bruise begins to form. The problem is a bruise on the hand can be seen while a bruise on the brain is invisible. It's like someone with fibromyalgia or Lyme's disease. There aren't a lot of discernable symptoms but inside, the person is experiencing a nightmare. That's what trauma does to a person, and you have been more than bruised between losing your parents and your home. Even moving to a new area is traumatic in its own way. Nobody knows that anything is wrong until something happens outwardly, like a person acting out or withdrawing into himself or herself. Believe me, I have seen it all. When a horrific act occurs out in the world by someone or some people, everyone immediately focuses on the victims, which they should, but I also go the extra mile of wanting to know why that person or group acted the way that they did."

"Are you saying I have post-traumatic stress syndrome?" Renee pointedly asked.

"I am not a psychiatrist or family doctor, but I have guests who are diagnosed with it. I can say this much that it would not be a bad idea to speak to your primary physician regarding this conversation, or you could sign a release for me to speak with him or her. I can say with confidence that trauma has profoundly affected you, but the fact that you came to see me today is the first step in moving forward and rebuilding your goals and dreams."

"I just want to save my motel and be strong for my family. They deserve a stable wife and mom."

"Then let's begin the rebuilding process."

Chapter 19

Memorial Weekend was rapidly approaching. I know from living in a high tourism area that the Memorial Day holiday is an extremely active one that signifies the dawn of a bustling summer season. The steamboat cruise ships were ready for new and returning passengers, and restaurants and bars were hiring additional staff and preparing inventory. Heather was already in her new position as evening bar manager at the Paddlewheel and loving every minute of it. She had been more attentive and chummy to me these last few weeks, especially since her mother has been working on her new plan affectionately known to us as "Save Serenity Savor." My new friends, Kevin and Nikki, booked the whole Memorial Weekend because they loved their stay here so much a couple of weeks ago. I did hang out with them after my meeting that day with Renee, and we wound up having dinner together at one of my favorite Italian restaurants in the town called Mario's. I love their chicken parmesan, and they have the best bread ever. I could just have a meal of bread baskets from there. Heather also invited me and my new friends to hang out at the Paddlewheel that weekend after my shift ended at eleven. I was really looking forward to it all.

Renee asked me to work all three nights that weekend, but that I could have the actual holiday off. She had also given me an extra night during the week as a regular shift. By the end of June, I should be full-time. Prior to this, I was getting ready to take another seasonal job if I wouldn't be at Serenity Savor for much longer, but it looks like I will be okay. Thank God.

When I was working on the Friday before Memorial Weekend, Derek checked in that evening. I hadn't seen him since opening weekend and I was getting concerned, especially since he told me he would be back. He had booked several weekends in advance, but he never called to cancel anything, so Renee left everything as it was. Even Heather stated it was out of character for him to do this, pardon the pun. When he walked in, I was overjoyed.

"Hey, stranger!" I called out.

Derek dropped his luggage on the floor, came around the desk, and crushed me in a bear hug.

"How are you, my friend? I missed you!"

"I missed you too! Where have you been? All of us were worried."

Derek was nonchalant about it. He shrugged and stated, "I needed to attend to a few other matters. Sometimes life happens, but I am here now, and starting next weekend I will be here for the whole season. You'll get sick of seeing me."

"Never!" I said, giving him a friendly punch in the arm. The house door opened and out walked Renee. She was wearing a really nice outfit; one I have never seen before.

"Oh my gosh, Derek! Our long-lost clown!"

Renee practically jumped in his arms, she was so ecstatic to see him. He was surprised to see her so jubilant.

"You look great, Renee! I am blushing over all of you missing me so much."

"We have. Well, I would love to chat, but I have an appointment I need to go to. Sage, you have my number if you need me."

"Yes, I do." I wondered what appointment she was going to. She didn't mention anything to me. I knew it wasn't our mutual therapist Erika because she just saw her two days ago. I hoped everything was all right. When Renee left, Derek turned to me with a questioning look.

"So much has been happening the last few weeks, actually since the last time you were here. It's good stuff, though."

"Well, I want to hear all about it, so why don't I get checked in and put all of this gear away? I'll come back down and we can chat."

"You probably have one suitcase just full of red noses," I joked.

"That reminds me," he stated, pulling something out of his shirt pocket. "I have one for you. Put it on!" he said, handing me a red nose.

"Now?"

"I want to see it on you."

So here I was with a red nose on my face. Derek instantly approved. If only Heather and Renee could see this.

"When something gets you down, you just put that on and look at yourself in the mirror. It will make you feel better."

"Or very silly." I stated, with a grin.

"Silly is good. It takes the stress away. Alright, let's get settled here."

As Derek took out his wallet, the phone rang. I picked it up and asked the person to hold since I had a guest checking in. Derek encouraged me to take the call, so I did. It was a reservation for Memorial Weekend, which was great. Renee was about three-quarters full, and while she was encouraged by this, reservations were still very low through the Labor Day weekend. She was working on the plan, though, since our conversation a few weeks ago.

"You're a natural." Derek stated.

"On the phone?"

"For this job. You are so good with people."

"I really love what I do. I enjoy meeting new people and hearing their stories. Of course, there have been a few crazy situations, but that goes with the territory."

"Oh yeah? Like what?"

"Well, one lady came flying into the office like she was being chased by a lion or something and yelled that she had an emergency in her room. Here I was ready to call 911, and then she mentioned that her toilet was overflowing all over the room. When I tried to nicely explain to her that it wasn't exactly an emergency, she proceeded to go into detail about what was floating around on the floor and destroying everything."

Derek was almost doubled-over with laughter.

"I told Renee about it later, and we both thought it made for a good Sci-Fi flick. The Invasion of the Floating Poop."

Now he lost it. Derek had to sit down and compose himself. I was laughing too.

"Another one was when Renee had an issue one night with her TVs. This couple came storming into the lobby and were very angry because they couldn't see the baseball game. I told them they could go to one of the local bars and see it there, but were they ever pissed! I still have difficulty with people yelling at me. Heather keeps telling me not to take it personally, but it brings me back to what I went through in my past."

"Nobody should be yelling at you, but unfortunately it does happen. People are lucky and blessed enough to be on vacation or a weekend away, and they let trivial matters upset them. I once had a lady push me down on the ground because she didn't like the way I face-painted her kid."

"Are you serious?" I was incredulous.

"Yup. Another time some guy threatened me because he felt I was checking out his girlfriend too much. How the heck did he even know where I was looking with the costume on? I mean, the eyes on my mask only go in one direction!"

"Oh my gosh, that's too much!"

"I try to put myself in their shoes and wonder why they are acting the way they are, but it does get hard at times."

There was wisdom to what Derek was saying.

"Well, let me get settled, and then you can fill me in on what's been going on at my summer home."

It was interesting what Derek said about being in other people's shoes because my therapist discussed the same issue with me last time I saw her. I finally broke down and filled her in about my older sister Kendra. Erika gave me an extra hour but did not charge me any more than what I was paying her. That's just who she is. I told her a lot about what happened while Kendra was at home, her disappearing, and then the phone call that I got on opening day. I described the whole scene that played out with Glen and the slapping. I told her I had nightmares about that for a week. I told her I felt so powerless. Erika was so loving and compassionate about how it affected me, but because she is a therapist, she needs to challenge me on new feelings and perspectives. She stated that while it was horrifying for me to hear what Glen was doing to Kendra, we had no idea what happened to Glen in his past to make him act out that way. We weren't there, so we can't understand the whole situation. I told Erika I am not at that point to feel sorry for Glen, yet. Erika said there was no timeline on recovery from any situation, but that it was important to keep working on it every day. We didn't speak about Renee directly, but Erika mentioned that she was thrilled with her new referral by me. I told her I would refer all of Lake George and upstate New York to her if I could.

Derek came back down a half-hour later and offered to pick up a pizza for us to share. It was almost seven, and I was hungry so I agreed. He left to pick up our order, and I attended to another matter. I placed a call to Gia's boyfriend, Evan. One of the suggestions we gave to Renee was to get a totally new website. What she had was so outdated, and she didn't have the technological skills to maintain it properly. Heather was more tech-savvy, but she had more than enough on her plate to contend with. She was also worried about the cost. Evan works as a website designer, and his work is excellent! He has clients all over the United States and internationally. Gia said he has an office in Glens Falls, but he also works from home, which he is tending to do more often now. She expressed concern that his work may be suffering too due to trying to handle everything with his family. Gia was pretty confident he would help Serenity Savor because it was me asking. I had another reason for reaching out, but right now, the website was primary concern. I called Evan's cell number. He answered right away, which I was surprised.

"Hey, Sage! How are you? Gia mentioned you may be calling."

At least they were still talking, that was a good sign.

"Do you have some time next week to meet? I have a work-related question for you."

He didn't hesitate. "For you, I have all of the time in the world. Why don't you meet me at my Glens Falls office on Monday at eleven? Does that work?"

"That works for me." I wrote it down on a post-it note.

"Okay, Sage. I look forward to it. Hey, I wanted to let you know Gia and I are going out tomorrow night. We are going to Ridge Terrace. You know how she loves it there."

Ridge Terrace is an amazing restaurant in a nearby town. It's a beautiful log-cabin atmosphere with the most amazing dishes. I was so happy they were going out on a date. I told Evan I would see him on Monday morning. I sent a text to Gia informing her that I just got off the phone with Evan and to have an amazing time the next night. I also mentioned I was meeting with him on Monday morning at eleven regarding the website issue. She texted back ten minutes later that she was so happy we connected, and that she was thrilled about their date. She was planning on bringing up Fourth of July, too, because she needed to let her bosses know whether she was taking her vacation then or not. I prayed it would all go well.

Chapter 20

Derek returned with a large plain pizza with a side order of garlic knots and a 2 cans of lemon iced tea. I wasn't expecting anyone else to check in unless someone came in off the street, and Renee still hadn't returned home yet. In between slices of pizza, I shared with Derek everything that took place the last few weeks. Renee gave me prior permission to share with him next time he came to the motel because he was the initial person she confided in. I did not mention that Renee was seeing a therapist; that was a personal matter that should be disclosed by her. I told him about my meeting with Evan about the website. He thought that was a fantastic idea.

"Websites and social media are the new way to advertise." he stated with conviction.

"Also, networking. She really hasn't gotten to know a lot of the local business owners personally. Even the crew at the Hungry Laker have heard of her, but never met her face-to-face."

"I'm surprised because Renee is so amazing with her guests. She goes out of the way to do so much for them."

"But that's here where she feels safe and comfortable. It takes a lot to go out and meet other people. She's been through a lot in her life."

"You really seem to know a lot about public relations."

I laughed to myself. "I guess part of it comes from my being a special-needs teacher. You have to constantly come up with new ways of reaching these children, and sometimes you need to seek out advice and guidance from others. Our principal was very big on in-services. I always enjoyed those."

As if on cue, Renee walked in with about five shopping bags. I can tell she hit the outlets. She also had her hair trimmed shorter. We both looked at her, eyebrows raised.

"Retail therapy?" Derek chimed.

"Nope. It was time for a change. I decided that as I go out to meet other business owners, I need to freshen up the look a bit. Heather has a coworker whose sister is a hairstylist, so she arranged an appointment for me. She works near the outlets, so I also decided to spruce up my wardrobe. I have too many jeans and cotton tops. Besides, Keith likes it when I get dressed up."

She turned away a little, blushing. I didn't say anything, but deep down I was thrilled for her. She was definitely making progress. She showed us her selections: a couple of skirts, blouses, and a dress. I have never seen Renee wear a dress before. They were in very bold colors too. I told her way back that Erika believes wearing bold clothes provides a feeling of confidence no matter how you are really feeling inside. She also said bold and bright colors are fantastic for any body type, which is good news for me.

"You have great taste," said Derek, approvingly.

"I have a great sales eye too. I couldn't believe the bargains I got for all of this. I am a happy camper."

She eyed the spread in front of her.

"Would you like some pizza or a garlic knot?" I offered.

"I will take some pizza, but I have to get back to regular cooking. I've been staying away from it for a while. Did you fill Derek in?" This was directed to me.

"Yes, but not everything." Renee knew what I meant.

"I don't care if Derek knows. I started seeing a counselor."

Derek nodded with compassion. He put a hand gently on her arm.

"She is the most caring and spiritual soul. I have seen her twice now, and I have already been feeling more hopeful. I didn't realize how depressed and disillusioned I had become with life. I also made an appointment with my primary physician to discuss other options. I am very holistic, so he suggested I try to get in a walk each day or yoga or something like that. He did prescribe a medication which I was open to during all of this change, but I don't want to be on it forever. I am trying."

Derek put an arm around her. "You're doing fantastic, my dear."

"And this one," Renee said, pointing at me, "has been an angel in disguise. I can't tell you how this motel has been blessed with her presence. I actually got on my knees the other night and thanked God for bringing Sage to Serenity Savor. Something has definitely changed here."

I felt it, too. Ever since that day I stepped onto the little beach and saw the guy with the metal detector, it was like a portal in the universe opened. My life felt like it was over back then, and in a lot of ways it was, but there was a new and different one just waiting for me to embrace it. Little did I know God would use me to help rebuild someone else's life in the process. You just never know.

"I made an appointment with my friend's boyfriend for Monday about the website." I reported.

"Oh good! Yeah, that thing is ancient. Heather swears she saw Vikings on it the other day. Leave it to my daughter, right? Well, whatever he can do to make it current would be most appreciated. On Sunday I am going to meet some of the other motel owners around here while Heather is on shift. Try to get some ideas."

I was so stoked to see Renee this excited and hopeful. She spent a few more minutes with us and then went into the house. I only had a couple of more hours before my shift ended. Derek went to his room around ten to prepare for the next day, but said that he would see me the following night. Everything seemed to be falling into place. I just wish the same would happen for Gia. I heard my cell phone ringing, and that same number with the exchange Kendra called me from was displayed. I decided to answer it. It was probably some telemarketer trying to scam me out of my life savings. *Good luck with that*, I thought.

"Hello?"

"Is this Sage Knight?" came a booming male voice. It sounded familiar. *No…it couldn't be*, I thought, as I considered who the voice sounded like.

"G-Glen?" I stammered. My heart started pounding.

"Is your sister with you?" He yelled so loud that I had to hold the phone away from my ear.

"Kendra? No, of course not! What's going on?" I demanded with more courage than I actually felt.

"She left me! She packed her shit and just left! Said she was going back to you!"

"Well, she isn't here, and I haven't heard from her since the night you slapped the crap out of her."

"I would do the same to you, you lying bitch! Now tell me where she is!"

Tears came to my eyes, and I was feeling short of breath. This was bringing back too much pain for me. I used an expression with Glen that involved a word I normally would never use, but I didn't care. Then, I hung up on him and raced upstairs to Derek's room. I pounded on the door. When he opened it, I grabbed hold of him and sobbed uncontrollably. Derek managed to close the door and wrapped his arms around me. He stroked my hair and rocked me back and forth.

"Sage, what happened? Oh my gosh, did someone hurt you?"

I couldn't even talk; I was so beyond distraught that I couldn't stop crying. Derek didn't ask me any more questions. He just let me get out all of the deep-seeded anguish that had been buried within me. It was like an invisible dam just burst inside of me, and Glen's words were the sledgehammer. There was another knock at the door. It was Renee.

"Sage? Sage, are you in there?"

"Renee, she is, but something happened. I don't know what, but she is in no shape to talk right now."

"Alright, I will watch the desk. It's almost eleven anyway. Sage, I hope you are okay! Call me tomorrow." She sounded really worried.

Nothing was okay. Nothing made sense. Derek gently held me away from him and cradled my face. I started feeling a little calmer.

"I'm sorry for bursting in on you like that." I whispered.

"Shh, shh, don't even give it a second thought. You did the right thing. I'm just thankful I was here. Let me get you some water."

He grabbed one of the plastic cups next to his ice bucket and filled it with water. He loves the room with the king bed and lake view. If I was a guest, I would have selected this room to stay in, too. I blew my nose because it was running like a sieve. I sat on the edge of the bed, and Derek sat on the recliner chair that was in the corner. He seemed to sense that I needed space to collect myself. I was so mortified, among other emotions.

"Just what Renee needs. Her night shift clerk falling apart on her."

"I think Renee would understand. Sage, what happened after I left?"

I haven't mentioned Kendra in years; now all of a sudden she was a hot topic, and I didn't want her to be. I had to tell Derek. I had the courage to speak with Erika about her, and she encouraged me to confide in Gia and other friends. Gia had enough going on without my adding to her drama, but Derek was a different story. For some reason I felt he would understand.

"How much time do you have?" I asked him.

"As long as it takes. I am here."

Chapter 21

The next morning, I woke up with a pounding headache. Thank God it wasn't a particularly sunny day out because my eyeballs wouldn't have been able to handle it. I was still dressed in my clothes. My eyes were still crusty and red from all of the tears shed just a few hours ago. I literally dragged myself out of bed. I normally make my bed, but this morning I didn't care. I shuffled over to the stove and put on the tea kettle. I wouldn't even look in the mirror; I didn't want to scare myself, or break the glass. When the kettle whistled, I poured the water in my favorite mug, which was a white one with smiley faces and a spiritual saying that read "Turn Your Scars into Stars" by Pastor Robert Schuller. Then, I took my tea and settled in my recliner. I kept all of the shades drawn, I wasn't ready to face the world yet.

I poured my emotional guts out to Derek last night. I shared stuff with him that even Erika wasn't privy to. I shared the whole ugly scenario regarding Glen beginning with the phone call on opening day through last night. I told him that it wasn't even just about my sister; it brought back horrible memories from being bullied in school and other settings. I disclosed about a notably upsetting memory where I was on the school playground and one girl who had it in for me called me these disgusting names and bent my arm behind my back, practically breaking it. I stated that when Glen called me a bitch, it exploded something inside of me. I told him the hotel that puts on the Hawaiian show in the area could have used me as part of the show because virtual lava was shooting out of my head. I then told Derek something that could have scared him off or turned him away from me, but he never faltered; I told him that when I get that angry, I have sometimes hurt myself through scratching my skin with a sharp object. I never understood that part of me until I admitted it to Erika. She, like Derek, never even flinched or acted like she thought I was crazy. Erika explained to me that it was pain I could control while there was so much going on around me that I felt powerless over. Every session since then, Erika checks in with me to how I have been coping and to learn new skills of dealing with my reactions in healthier ways. One of them was to reach out to a safe person immediately following the triggering episode. Since I didn't want to burden Gia, Derek was the next logical choice. He was so moved that I trusted him enough to unload all of this, and he never took advantage of anything. He just listened. He should be a clown/counselor.

I glanced over at the cat clock on the wall, it was an old-fashioned one; where the eyes and tail move back and forth. It was after ten. I should call Renee and let her know I was okay. I was so embarrassed that I left the desk, and it wasn't fair to Renee or Heather. They can't keep covering for me every time I have a meltdown or something goes wrong in my life. They have their problems too and yet manage to keep going. It's time for me to step up to the plate and really work on rebuilding, whatever that looks like. I picked up my phone and dialed Renee's mobile. She answered right away.

"Hey, Sage! I was just going to call you. Are you home?"

"Yes, I am, but…"

She didn't let me finish. "I need you to help me with something. I will be over in twenty minutes. See ya!"

I stared at the phone wondering what just happened, but then my brain cells unscrambled enough to register that my boss was coming to my apartment in now-nineteen minutes, and I was still in the same clothes I wore on shift last night. I ran into my room, grabbed whatever was first available and ran to the bathroom. One of my superpowers is that I can choose an outfit, shower, and get dressed in ten minutes. Growing up in a house with four family members and one bathroom led to this. I slacked in the makeup area a little at this time, but at least I was wearing different clothes and smelled decent.

Renee knocked on my door at 10:40AM. When I opened it, I was overcome by strong, delicious aromas coming from a basket in her arms.

"WOW, that smells awesome!"

"Oh good! I was hoping for that response. May I come in?"

"Of course." I stepped aside and let her enter. Renee put the mystery basket down on my small round table that was technically my dining room table. It was fine because, with the exception of Gia or my parents visiting, I don't have need for a bigger one to entertain. Renee removed a thick red dish towel and revealed cinnamon buns and some kind of muffin or muffins.

"Try one!" Renee encouraged. She looked excited.

I helped myself to a cinnamon bun, which was drizzled with cream cheese icing. These were even better than the ones at our meeting a few weeks ago, if that was possible.

"Try a muffin too."

I did as I was told. It was a banana muffin. If it's possible to get the same feeling from food that comes after having sex, these would do the trick.

"Oh my gosh, these are sooooo delicious!"

"Really? You're not just saying that?"

"No, I really love them! These are even more delicious than the ones we ate that day we went over the marketing plan."

"I made some changes. Well, you inspired me."

I almost choked on a piece of cinnamon bun. "Me?"

Renee sat down on my couch. I took some paper plates, picked up the basket, and walked over to where Renee was.

"Remember when you said that what I baked was so good that I should make it available at the continental breakfast? At first, I was totally against the idea because I was in a bad place in my head. What is it called, stinking thinking? Erika taught me that. She said I need to get my head back from down below to all the way up here, where it belongs."

I smiled. That sounds like Erika.

"Anyway, I thought about what you said that day, and decided I am going to try it out. In fact, I am experimenting Memorial Weekend."

I sat straight up. This was big news.

"That's fantastic!"

"It will help keep costs down, too. Keith said to me a few nights ago that I should bake in bulk rather than buying packages and boxes of store-bought goods. I am also cutting back on the bagels for now. I have a lot of my mom's recipes from when she baked for the guests. That was another reason I didn't want to do it. It was painful to be reminded of my childhood, even though it was a good memory."

I nodded and understood more than she realized.

"Which brings me to my next question. I will need some extra help with preparing all of these goodies. If you're available, would you mind coming over for a few hours on Friday morning to help prepare muffins? The buns I can make early in the morning Saturday and Sunday. I realize you are working the three shifts next weekend, but we can work something out."

Renee didn't have to ask me twice. With all that she has done for me and been through, it was the least I could do. I told her I would be there with bells on. It would be fun, too.

"Awesome! I really appreciate it. I made some changes since the other ones, so I think I will stick with what I did with these guys." she said, pointing at the basket.

I wasn't sure whether to bring up last night, but I felt I should. I wanted to reassure her.

"Renee, about last night..."

Renee put a hand on my arm. "Sage, it's okay. I don't know what happened, and I don't need to know. Look, we are all dealing with mega-crap from our pasts. I am the last one who should pass judgment. I turned into a recluse without even realizing it, and next thing I know my motel is in jeopardy of closing. My family has suffered because of it, but thank God I am taking steps now to change things. Just like you are."

It didn't feel like it at the moment.

"I know you are an excellent worker. The guests that we have had reported wonderful feedback about you. That's music to my ears since the whole Roxanne fiasco."

That warmed my heart. I had no idea.

"We are all human and trying to do the best we can each day. Nobody's perfect, last I checked. We need to support each other as we grow."

I felt Renee was making way more progress than me, and she has only been in therapy for a couple of weeks!

"We have a big weekend coming up, my friend. This is our time to make magic. It's the beginning of summer tourism. Let's make some amazing memories for our guests!"

"Amen to that!" I shouted, as Renee and I high-fived each other.

Chapter 22

I was driving to Evan's office in Glens Falls. The weather was still cloudy and gray, but it wasn't raining today. Yesterday it poured buckets. I suspected Gia's tears were part of that rainstorm, as she called me in the afternoon in tears. She and Evan did go on their date to Ridge Terrace Saturday night and had an amazing time, but then he took her by the lake and had a serious talk about where things stood with his family. Evan admitted he just wasn't ready to make the decision to have his mother moved from their home for more advanced care. He said in his family they handle everything within the home, and if need be they will hire more help. He said he loved Gia so much, but he couldn't walk away from his parents at this time. Gia did not handle this too well and told him she needed time and space to process everything. Here she thought he might pop the question, but instead it felt more like a breakup. Gia decided to take her vacation in early June and go somewhere on her own because she needed to get away and try to figure things out. I felt sick for both of them.

I didn't hear from Evan about whether he could still meet with me, so I assumed the appointment was still on. I pulled into the parking lot of the brick building where his office was located. I noticed a lot of homes and businesses were adorned in flags and patriotic banners in preparation for the holiday weekend. My landlord puts out a big flag every year at this time and keeps it out through September 11th in honor of all of the memorials and holidays. I have a candolier in my bedroom window and depending on what time of the year it is I change the bulbs accordingly. Right now they are red, white, and blue and will stay that way through 09/11 as well. Paul had also informed me my new neighbors will be moving next door the week after Memorial Weekend. It will be nice to have company around.

I entered the building and took the elevator to the third floor. Evan's office was at the end of the hallway. His door was closed, so I knocked before entering. I heard a loud "Come in", so I opened the door. Evan was on the phone, but indicated I should take a seat. He had a nice plush dark blue chair in front of his desk, so I sat there until he was done with his call.

Evan is a very handsome and clean-cut Mexican-American man, and the first day I met him at Gia's, I wanted to know if he had a twin brother. He does have a brother, but he is married and living in Oregon. Today, he was dressed in a black pin-stripe suit, and I felt my heart flutter. I scolded myself because this was my best friend's boyfriend, but I would have to be six feet under to not appreciate the hunk of a man directly in front of me.

Evan ended his call and apologized that he couldn't respond to me right away.

"You have other clients. I know this is a favor you are doing for me, which I deeply appreciate."

Evan came around the desk, bent down and kissed my cheek. He then went to the coffee area. He still prefers to use a regular coffeepot as opposed to a Keurig. I don't care, as long as the coffee tastes good.

"You want some coffee? It's a fresh pot."

"Sounds great. Just ½ and ½, no sugar."

Evan brought my coffee over to me and then sat behind his desk. He looked really tired. Normally he is so upbeat like Gia. That's what attracted them to each other in the first place.

"I'm surprised you still came. I assume you know what happened the other night."

I nodded. "Not my position to judge."

"I think it may be over between us."

I spit coffee out. Evan handed me a tissue box. I was NOT expecting that!

"I don't believe that." I responded. More like I refused to.

"You weren't there. I have never seen that side of Gia, I literally thought she was going to shove me in the lake."

You would have deserved it, I thought angrily to myself.

"I don't know what else to do, Sage. I love Gia more than anything, but it's complicated."

"Well, obviously that's not true because you two are breaking up!"

Evan stared at me wide-eyed. I couldn't believe what I just said. I counted to ten, as Erika taught me to do, and then I spoke in a calmer voice.

"I apologize. That was very rude of me to say. You're doing this as a favor for me and taking time out of your day. But, in fairness, you rang the bell first."

Evan nodded and realized I was right. I had no intentions of bringing up his and Gia's situation, at least not in the beginning of the meeting, but he brought it up instantly.

"I don't know what to do, Sage. I love her so much, but I love my family too. I can't turn my back on them either."

I felt for Evan at that moment. I knew a little of what he was going through, but it still wasn't fair to Gia.

"Evan, do you want to hear what I have to say, or I am overstepping?"

He leaned forward with his hands clasped, as if he was praying.

"Please say anything you feel. I am at a loss."

I took a deep breath and began speaking. "When my marriage ended, it nearly killed me. When I got married, I really believed it would be forever. You know the details, so I won't get into all of that again, and your situation is totally different from mine. One thing I will share with you is that trouble begins when communication breaks down."

I got up and started pacing around, as this was diving into turbulent waters again.

"I can't even say when things began to fall apart, but it usually occurs when your spouse or significant other shuts you out of important matters and decisions, or is afraid to take a stand against certain beliefs and attitudes of the family." I continued.

I knew I was treading on volatile ground, but surprisingly Evan did not react. When he didn't say anything, I continued. I swallowed and took a breath.

"When a marriage ends friends and family immediately question why you got married in the first place. It's not really a fair question because even though the relationship fell apart, these were two people in love at one point. I loved my ex, but the road things went down was wrong. It doesn't matter whose fault it was; the fact is, somewhere along the way, some people forget what they loved about the other person or they get stuck trying to fix everything and everyone else in their personal lives. Problem is, they get so busy trying to be superheroes, they don't see who they have left behind."

"Is that what you and Gia think? That I am trying to be a superhero? Jesus, Sage, this is my mom! They're my parents!"

I knew Evan would get upset, but I had to keep going. I cared too much about them both, so I had to speak the truth no matter how much it hurt to hear. I turned around and faced Evan.

"Evan, we both know that. Gia would never expect you to turn your back on your parents. She just feels left out. Let me explain it this way, you know, I was an in-class support teacher. I was assigned a small group of kids who needed special instruction within a regular education classroom. Each child needed individual instruction. Now, some had more intense needs than others and, at times, required extra attention from me, but I still worked with my other kids no matter what. Can you imagine what would happen if I only worked with the ones who had deeper needs and ignored the others?"

Evan looked down, considering my words.

"And what about your job? I'm sure some clients require more effort than others, but does that mean you ignore your other clients?"

Evan took a sip of his coffee, appearing very pensive.

"Gia shared a comment with me that she doesn't want to be treated as a side dish. She deserves to be treated as the full entrée. I mean, when was the last time you two shared dessert?"

Evan raised his eyes at me and shook his head. That was their code for making whoopee.

"I know, it's none of my business, but that's exactly what I'm talking about. Gia wants to be involved with everything. Don't shut her out. She loves you, you big dope! Don't let what I am going through right now happen to you because, believe me, it's painful as hell."

Evan stood up, came over and hugged me. His eyes were full of tears.

"Thank you for being such an amazing friend, Sage. Thank you for your honesty. I'm such an idiot for letting Gia slip away like that. As soon as we finish our meeting, I am going to call her and ask to come by tonight. We really need to talk."

"I love you both."

"We love you too. And someday, Cupid will find you again."

I shrugged. "I like my independence right now. Starting a new career and everything. But, thank you for the thought."

Evan wiped his eyes. We both refilled our mugs.

"Alright, my dear, what can I do to help Serenity Savor?"

Chapter 23

Memorial Weekend was here. Lake George and its surrounding areas were ready to go and enthusiastically awaiting tourists from all over the world. There were tons of activities planned for the long weekend including festivals, concerts, and historical fort tours. I really love where I live. I have been to other states as I enjoy traveling in general, but the Adirondacks are my home. So many times when I needed time to regroup, I drove along the lake or spent time in one of the local parks. I feel a spiritual connection to the lake and mountains. My parents love it too, which made it even more painful when Kendra ditched us all. She always said she never fit in here. God only knows where she is now.

I worked from eight until twelve on Friday, helping Renee bake muffins for the weekend continental breakfast. Heather kept walking in and complaining the yummy smells were distracting her. We all laughed. Renee and I made banana, corn, and blueberry muffins. Because I worked four hours, she was allowing me to come in at four instead of three so I could rest a little before the shift. She even said that she would pay me for that hour, too. Renee said she would cover the extra hour until I came in. She was also ordering pizzas for us later. Keith was helping out the whole weekend because Memorial Weekend crowds can be a bit crazy, and he wanted to help keep an eye on things. I actually got to check out his ski lodge earlier this week, which was a lot of fun. I am trying to get out more, and I have never been to Adirondack

122

Lodge before. Keith introduced me to a lot of people. It was a really fun place, I can't imagine what the winters must be like there!

Keith took me aside when we were there and thanked me profusely for helping his wife come out of her shell. He said he hasn't seen this much excitement in her for years. Privately, he voiced his concern on whether the motel would survive, but he was encouraged by what was happening. He wanted it to for Renee's sake. So did I. Serenity Savor was much more than a job at this point; it had become like a family to me.

After my meeting with Evan on Monday, he reached out to Renee and the two got together at the motel on Tuesday. He came up with an incredible website for Serenity Savor, and both Renee and Heather were thrilled beyond belief. I already knew what he was capable of, but even I was blown away. As payment for his time, Renee comped her best room for him and Gia to spend the weekend there over July 4th. Evan and Gia did get together that evening after our talk, and I was so stoked to find out they were back together. Of course, Gia took up half of my Tuesday evening with the details, but I was so happy for my friends! Unfortunately, she couldn't change the June vacation, but they compromised for the Fourth of July so they would still be able to spend the entire weekend together. Apparently, Evan reached out to his brother that week too and poured his heart about what was going on. Evan's brother, Alex, agreed to come the holiday weekend and give Evan a much-needed break. The two brothers also agreed to discuss what was happening within the family once Fourth of July was over.

My new friends Kevin and Nikki were scheduled to arrive on Friday evening around 9:00PM. They took a room on the second floor and were excited that Renee had a sundeck. Kevin and Nikki enjoyed hanging out on the deck the last time they were here while they were drinking a bottle of wine, people-watching, and viewing the lake. I suggested to Evan and Renee that they advertise the sundeck because it was a nice perk of staying there. Evan went a step further to including pictures of actual guests sitting there with beverages and food, with their permission of course, and included a spectacular view of the lake in the back. He took the pictures at sunset, which added a divine angle to the setting. Renee loved them. He really knows his stuff!

Derek had an incredibly busy schedule. He was booked for events on some of the steamboats through Lake George Steamboat Company and Shoreline Cruises. He was also performing in a couple of festivals and walking in the Memorial Day Parade. I would most likely not see him that much, but we would all be very busy this weekend. Heather would be practically living at the Paddlewheel. Kevin, Nikki, and I would be going there tomorrow night after my shift to hear a band perform that Heather highly recommended. She also promised a free drink to each of us, which was a great incentive!

Renee was working feverishly to prepare for a successful weekend. All of the muffins were ready to go, and Renee would be up at the crack of dawn preparing the cinnamon buns. Besides coffee, she bought a bulk amount of small juices to have available. Keith learned the basics of the reservation program so he could help cover Heather in the early morning since she was working so late at the bar. Everyone was working together to help pull a Lazarus for Serenity Savor. Before I arrived at four, I got down on my knees and prayed that this weekend would soar for Renee because she deserved a miracle. I also thanked the Lord for bringing me to the motel. It wasn't the life I planned, but it doesn't mean it can't be good again.

Heather was pumped about the weekend. As Renee told me, she thrives on crowds. Renee also told me privately that Heather was definitely planning to start school the following January. In the fall, Heather plans to check out hotels in some of the big cities to get an idea of where she would like to work permanently. She will have no problem getting a position with her experience and drive.

From four to seven, it was non-stop. Guests were constantly coming through to check in, and the phones were non-stop. Renee helped with answering phones and greeting guests. Keith took care of minor maintenance issues because there was no way I could leave the desk to attend to anything. At seven-thirty Keith picked up a bunch of pizzas. I was famished by then. We all took turns eating. One of the guests pointed at the boxes when Keith and I were at the desk and joked, "Hey, you should have some for us tourists!"

Keith snickered, but it gave me an idea to discuss at a later time. I also needed to address the phone system issue. Renee really needs a portable phone.

"So," Keith began, "what did you think of the lodge?"

"It was awesome! Believe it or not, it was the first time I have ever been there even though I lived here all my life."

"You've never skied?" Keith questioned.

"I did when I was in youth group, but unfortunately I got injured. It was a shame because I really enjoyed it."

"Would you try it again?"

It was funny because Gia asked me the same thing when we got together.

"I think I'd like to, but I would need an instructor this time."

Keith held his arms open with the expression of 'what about me?'

"You would teach me?" I asked humbly.

"Of course! Actually, if you're interested, we need winter help at Adirondack. I have a lot of clout there. You'd be perfect."

"Not at the chair lifts! That'd be an accident waiting to happen. I fell off the darn thing and laid in the snow while they had to shut it down."

Keith laughed, hard. "Oh, my dear, you are not the only one that has done that. No, you would not be at the lifts. I would find you something with customer service since you're so great with people."

It is amazing how I did not feel this appreciated or valued at my previous job. It's part of the reason I got so sick. My gastroenterologist explained that diverticulitis is oftentimes brought on by stress. Between my personal and professional life at the time, it was a miracle I wasn't in the hospital longer than I was. Here at the motel I am constantly reminded how grateful they are for my help. I admit, I am not used to it and sometimes I wonder if the proverbial shoe will fall. Erika keeps telling me that I need to reframe my thinking and perception of myself because other people see so much good inside me, but she also understands how the multiple mental wounds have affected me and how I view things. As she says, I am a work in progress.

Nikki and Kevin arrived at 9:15PM. They both hugged me and were so excited about staying there again. I told them about the new continental breakfast, which they enthusiastically looked forward to. After I checked them in, Kevin invited me to sit with them on the sundeck and have some wine. I knew I would be too wired to go to sleep right away, so I agreed. By ten-thirty, everyone who made reservations was already checked in. We weren't full tonight, but it was close. The awesome news was Renee was booked the next two nights and half-full on Monday. She was very happy!

We had a couple of last-minute check-ins, so I didn't actually leave until 11:20PM, but my friends were still at the deck, holding onto the comforts of the night with good wine and great snacks. The town was so crowded! A lot of the younger crowds were hanging around, but that was expected this weekend. I hung out with Kevin and Nikki until 12:30AM, and then I walked back to my place. Overall, I felt tonight went really well. I just hoped it would continue.

Chapter 24

"OH MY GOD, WE DID IT!!"

This was Renee on Tuesday morning following the long holiday weekend. She was jumping up and down like a kid on Christmas morning. She sent a text to me on Monday night requesting me to stop by the motel on Tuesday morning around eleven. After three intense shifts, I crashed the whole day in my apartment. I stayed in my pajamas and got caught up on some of my reading. Normally I would have visited my parents, but they understood I was exhausted. Even Gia didn't text or call, but perhaps she and Evan were making up for lost time. I know she had the holiday off.

"This weekend was a success! We all did it!"

Heather was still sleeping. She deserved it, as she worked her ass off at both jobs over four days. She was supposed to have last night off, but two people called in sick at the Paddlewheel, and they were extremely short-staffed. Heather rose to the occasion and worked from six to midnight. I am sure she appreciated the extra money as well. Kevin, Nikki, and I did go there on Saturday night after eleven and had a blast! As promised, Heather treated us each to a free drink; I chose a screwdriver. The band was amazing! Nikki danced along with some other people. She tried to get me to dance, but I wasn't ready for that yet. Just being there was progress enough.

"So, now that we survived Memorial Weekend, we need to plan for the rest of the summer."

"Definitely keep the baked goods," I stated.

Renee's cinnamon buns and muffins were a mega-hit! We came very close to running out on Sunday morning, and a few people grumbled that we didn't have them available on Monday morning. Renee felt a bit bummed about it, but as Keith said, you can't please everyone. Plus, she needed a break.

"I would love to have them available every morning for the summer, but I don't know if that's possible with the financial situation right now."

"Plus, that's a lot on you to do that, honey." Keith said, sounding concerned.

"Um, someday I hope to run a bed-and-breakfast, so I better get used to it. Though, I would have more staff available, too."

Keith and I exchanged a knowing look. Renee hasn't mentioned the bed-and-breakfast dream in a while. That was a great sign.

"Well, except for a couple of kids trying to jump off the balcony into the pool, there were no incidents." Keith reported.

This apparently happened late Saturday night. Keith heard some ruckus outside and sure enough, he caught two twenty-some year-old boys attempting to dive into the pool from the second floor. Keith is very tall and fit so once he showed up, the show was over. They didn't cause a scene or give him a hard time, so they weren't thrown out. Keith actually found humor in it.

"You gotta admire their mojo." he said. Renee just rolled her eyes at him. They were so adorable together.

Kevin and Nikki had an absolute blast. In fact, they reserved the same room for July 4th and Labor Day weekends. They were planning on telling their friends and coworkers back in New Jersey to book at Serenity Savor. We exchanged phone numbers so we could chat until they come here again. It was wonderful bonding with my new friends.

Derek left early that morning for a clowning job somewhere near Lake Placid, but he had an incredibly active weekend as well. I only saw him briefly, but I did manage to thank him for being my shoulder and sounding board the weekend before. He asked me to come by one of his events sometime. He is here for the entire summer, so that will definitely be possible.

"So, Sage, do you have time to sit down with me and go over some ideas?"

I had nothing planned except for washing some dishes left over from the day before. That could definitely wait.

"Yes, I do."

"Great, take a seat."

Keith said he was going to work on the pool that morning, but then he needed to spend some time at the lodge in the afternoon. His boss needed Keith's input regarding some upcoming summer events. When he left, Renee looked in his direction with googly eyes.

"I love my man." she said adoringly. Then suddenly she got serious and stated, "Sage, I am so sorry. That must be so insensitive on my end."

Normally I would have been upset, but I was actually okay about it.

"Renee, it's fine. I confess it used to bother me when other people talked about their boyfriends, husbands, significant others, or whatever. Now it's not so bad. Don't forget my best friend is with Evan, although they just had some rocky times. Just because my relationship didn't work out doesn't mean I can't be happy for others whose marriages are on solid ground."

"Keith has been my rock. I have often asked him why he has put up with me for so long. He claims it's for my baked goods." she said with a wink.

"Yeah, I'm sure it's a lot more than that."

"Even when he came to me and said we may need to sell Serenity Savor, he wasn't like some men who would just tell it like it was with no affect or feeling for me. He had tears in his eyes when he talked about it because he knew how much this place means to me. Now there is a big flicker of hope again."

A tear rolled down Renee's cheek. I put a hand on her shoulder. There still was a long way to go but, as she said, there was hope now. We would just need to keep the momentum flowing.

"So, we have the website updated, which a lot of the customers remarked that they loved the new look. And we have my baked goods."

She was jotting down everything on a yellow legal pad.

"What else?" Renee asked, without looking up.

"A portable phone." I blurted out.

"What?"

"You need a portable phone."

"I had one of those a couple of years back. It got to be too expensive."

"Well, you need one again."

Renee shook her head. "Nope. Can't do it."

"Renee, it wasn't a big deal in the spring when it wasn't as busy, but we all could have used one this weekend. If it wasn't for you and Keith being able to take care of issues, I don't know how that would have worked out. I feel like I am stuck at the desk without one."

"So you just call me when you need to take care of a room issue, that's all. Heather does it all the time."

I was starting to feel a bit impatient. Renee wasn't seeing the big picture.

"Renee, it's not even just about problems in the room. What about being able to mingle with the guests? I would love to walk around and talk with people, and get to know them. More importantly, you should be doing that. No sooner do I get up from the desk to go to the bathroom or something, and the phone rings."

"Well, you wouldn't be talking on the phone in the bathroom!"

"No, but I can put them on hold! At least they're acknowledged. Renee, you asked me for help and suggestions. Sometimes you have to put out money to make money."

"Easy for you to say. Are you my financial advisor too?" Renee asked with a sneer.

I stood up, grabbed my purse and said, "I think we need a breather. We're both exhausted and not at our best. Let's table this for another time."

Before Renee could say anything else, I headed out the door. It was really starting to feel like summer. My red leather jacket was put away until next fall, I recently changed my hair color from dark brown to a vibrant red, and I also cut it shorter. Because my hair is so thick, the humidity drives me crazy. My hair winds up looking like I stuck my finger in a light socket. I didn't feel like going back to the apartment yet, so I took a walk. There were still some tourists in the area extending their holiday into the week. I walked to the park by the beach area and sat down in one of the Adirondack chairs under a big tree. I watched people walk by and ducks float on the water. In another couple of weeks, the lake would soon be filled with boats and parasailers. I have parasailed in the past, and loved it. I leaned back in the chair and closed my eyes. There was a slight breeze blowing.

The side of Renee I just saw is not easy to deal with, but then I have not always been a piece of cake, either. I know myself enough that I can overreact very strongly when I feel attacked, so I am learning to walk away instead of attack back. In truth, Renee was right. I had no business telling her what to do with her money, but it's something my uncle always said. He would know as he built a very lucrative career on that principle. I was just trying to help.

A couple of hours later, I headed back to my place. Paul's pick-up truck was there. He was getting everything ready for the new family arriving next week. He told me that they were a couple with two girls and a boy.

"Hey, Knight! I see you survived the craziness!"

"Yup. It actually went well, but I didn't move out of the apartment yesterday."

"I bet. If you hear anything downstairs, I am staying here through the weekend. Need to get prepared for my new tenants."

Paul keeps the downstairs apartment for himself to use in preparation of situations like this. He has a cabin somewhere further north where he spends the majority of his time.

"So, what are the new people like?"

Paul set down some materials and stated, "Very nice family. It was a rough area where they were living, so this will be a welcoming space for them. The husband and wife are Kyle and Denise DaSilva, and the children are Daryl, Amy, and Aaron."

"Nice. I look forward to meeting them."

"They have a hedgehog too, I know that."

"Oh, cute!" I love animals.

"Well, you may hear a lot of noise the next few days. I won't hammer into the night, though."

I knew Paul wouldn't anyway, but that was nice of him to assure me. Before he stepped inside the house, I called out to him.

"Hey, Paul!"

"Yes, Knight?"

I picked up one of his tools, held it up high and stated, "I have rebuilt!"

Paul gave me a big smile and nodded approvingly.

"I had no doubt you would. And you continue to rebuild and update. I am so proud of you, Knight. You will do amazing things. Just keep the faith."

I went inside so Paul could continue his work for the day. I looked out the window towards Serenity Savor. It's hard to believe that only three short months ago, I was on that little beach by the lake in tears wondering where my life was heading. Now, I am in a new career that I strongly believe I didn't choose for myself; I do believe it chose me.

Chapter 25

It was the end of June, and we were in preparation mode for July 4th weekend. I was now full-time on the night shift. My days off were Thursday and Sunday. My parents finally met my new boss, and Renee was gracious enough to let them use the pool whenever they wanted. I even took advantage of it myself. It's heated and feels like a bathtub. I was starting to get some color, though I don't often suntan that much because of skin cancer worries.

Renee wound up reaching out to me the next day after our disagreement. She called Erika and explained what happened, so Erika did a phone session with her. Renee realized she was letting fear take over, and she was so scared of losing more money that she felt she had to hold whatever she had prisoner. She talked it over with Heather, who immediately agreed that a portable phone was necessary, especially with future growth. So, Renee bit the bullet and obtained a basic one until their situation improved.

At first, it took a while for guests to get used to the portable set-up. The blue phone on the desk was previously hooked up to a phone inside the house, so Renee would always know when someone was at the desk. Now, it was hooked up to the portable. It's actually been quite humorous at times. One day I had to go in the basement for some extra linens and the portable rang in my pocket. When I answered, the voice on the other end stated, "There's nobody at the front desk."

Now, I could have been sarcastic and said "Really? I was just there a second ago!" Instead, I professionally stated that I was on the portable phone and would be there momentarily. Another time, Renee and I were in the house and this guy walked up to the desk in front of the sign that clearly stated the instructions. Instead of following them, he started yelling hello and then wound up drumming on the desk. We finally took pity on the man and came out to the lobby. When he was going on about nobody being there, Renee gently moved the sign and asked, "I assume you read the sign." The dude's face turned beat red, and he didn't say another word about it. It has come in really handy, though, and Renee just admitted not too long ago that she was so happy I pushed her to get one again.

Renee's numbers were steadily picking up. The weekends in June were really packed, especially for a mammoth motorcycle event that takes place in Lake George this time every year. We were booked solid for that one. Evan loves that event because he rides a Harley himself. He wants to teach Gia how to ride one. For now, she is content riding on the back as a passenger hanging onto him.

She still wasn't having as many reservations during the week in June, but July and August were definitely better. Evan checks in with Renee every week about anything new she wants to add on her website. We recently got Serenity Savor on some of the big social media sites as well. I love to take pictures with my phone, so I went over one day and snapped a bunch of them. I then went over them with Renee and Heather, and they selected which ones they preferred for their social media pages. Things were definitely on the upswing.

One morning I went to the Hungry Laker for breakfast. I hadn't been there in a while, so Ally was thrilled to see me.

"You look fantastic, Sage! I haven't seen you in a while. I love your hair!"

"Thank you. It was time for a change, I love red. To me, it signifies boldness and confidence, which I don't always feel."

"I hear ya on that. Well, enjoy your breakfast. Great to see you!"

Ally was always so cheerful. I wasn't going to look at the menu because I was in the mood for Eggs Benedict, but something inside convinced me I should. When I opened the menu, I had an idea wash over me. I knew then why I was supposed to look. When Ally walked by to seat another person, I asked her to stop by my table. When she did, I asked, "Ally, how come you guys don't have many baked goods?"

Ally sat down across from me.

"We used to have a baker on staff, but we caught her stealing from the till. After that, Shannon couldn't find anyone to replace her."

Shannon was the owner of the café. I asked if she was in yet, but she wasn't. I ran my idea by Ally, who thought it was a fantastic suggestion.

"I know Shannon will be in before I leave for the day. I will run this by her. I'm excited!"

I wonder if Renee will be open to it, I thought.

Breakfast was awesome, as usual. I got a text from Gia that she and Evan were really looking forward to staying at Serenity Savor for the 4th of July. Evan booked a dinner cruise on one of the steamboats for Sunday that weekend and wanted me to join them. He offered to pay my ticket since he felt indebted to me for helping restore their relationship. I thought it was a bit unusual that they wanted me with them, but they both insisted. I texted

Gia back that I accepted and to thank Evan for paying for my ticket. She texted back with a smiley heart emoji.

I took a stroll by the lakefront where the boats were and saw a crowd not too far from the Fort William Henry Hotel. I wasn't sure what was going on, so I walked over to take a closer look. Lo and behold, it was my good friend Minno, aka Derek. He was entertaining a lot of giggly children and curious adults. He was making balloon animals and doing face-painting. I was getting a huge kick out of watching him. Wouldn't you know, he spots me in the back of the crowd and calls me over to the front. I tried to avoid going, but by then everyone knew it was me he zeroed in on. I had no choice but to go forward. *He owes me for this one*, I thought. When I was right next to him, he whipped out one of his famous red noses and stuck it right on my nose. *Well, at least the kids love it*, I thought. Then, he took out two more and stuck one on my right ear and the other on the left ear. By then, the kids and their parents are in hysterics. The laughter was so loud, other people started coming over to see what the commotion was about. I had to admit, it was funny. Then he started putting stickers all over my face. I had no idea what they were, but they were making the kids go crazy with laughter. At that moment, I felt a wave of peace come over me that I couldn't explain. Six months ago I would have run in tears or felt so humiliated by what was going on. I remember Heather confronting me the first day I worked the night shift about having a perfectionistic personality. She was absolutely on point. I wanted to appear perfect, like everything was hunky-dory in my life. I didn't want the "red noses" of my life showing on my face, or anywhere for that matter. I didn't want to feel exposed, so I hid. Ironically, that's what Renee had been doing too, and God knew we could help each other. I concluded that I did not have to be afraid to be silly or vulnerable; I just needed to be me.

Chapter 26

"Well, Renee, a lot has changed for you, hasn't it?" Erika asked.

It was July 1st, the Friday before another big weekend in Lake George. Erika normally didn't work on Fridays, but she was going on vacation for two weeks and she wanted to make time for Renee, especially since so much had transpired. Erika still served Renee her coffee and enjoyed a cup with her as well.

"Erika, I can't believe how much has changed. I don't even know where to begin. Do you know I am actually full all three nights this weekend?"

"Woohoo!" Erika high-fived Renee. "That's amazing!"

"I haven't been full for this weekend for years. Labor Day isn't looking so bad either."

"So, tell me what has been going on."

Erika knew about the website and social media pages. She also knew Renee bought a new portable phone, per their mutual friend's suggestion.

"Erika, I was so against it, but thank God I listened to you, Sage, and everyone else. I felt I had to penny-pinch everything. Plus--- and I will only admit this to you right now---not having a portable phone was an excuse for me to remain hidden."

Erika nodded, knowingly. "I am not surprised."

"It gave me a false sense of control, but as Sage pointed out, it was keeping her and all of us from effectively doing our jobs. There was another perk too with it, as we found out."

"Oh yeah, what's that?"

"Sage took the phone in the bathroom with her, as she always does. She left her cell in the drawer. Well, the door handle got stuck, and poor Sage got locked in the bathroom. She had to call me to come rescue her."

Erika lost it. "That's hysterical!"

"Sage shook the phone in my face and said it was a good thing we had this thing now. I had to admit, she was right. Plus, it gave me a good laugh at her expense." Renee said, winking.

"What else has been going on besides your desk clerks getting locked in the bathroom?"

"Well, this is a biggie. Sage got me hooked up with a café owner in the village of Lake George. Sage noticed they didn't have a lot of baked goods on their menu, which she asked about. It turns out that the previous baker stole from them."

Erika sat back. "Well, that just gives new meaning to sticking your hands in the cookie jar, doesn't it?"

Renee laughed and shook her head. "Yes, it does. Well, Sage suggested that perhaps the owner and I could work out a deal with me baking for them. I have been providing my own baked goods for the continental breakfast, which have been going over extremely well, so I told Shannon that I could make extras for her. She jumped on it because supposedly word has gotten around the village that my cinnamon buns are the best out there."

"That's unreal. Truly amazing."

"We worked out the financial details that benefitted us both; plus, now we offer a special that if you stay two nights at my motel, you receive a 25% off voucher at the Hungry Laker."

"The power of networking."

"The extra income has really been a tremendous blessing. I am not out of the dark completely, but there is a huge light at the end of the tunnel."

Erika leaned forward again. "And you will get to that light. I know how hard it was for you to confront those demons of the past. I can't tell you how proud I am of you. This is only the beginning. I have no doubt that Serenity Savor will rise again from the ashes."

Renee looked down.

"What is it, Renee?"

"What you just said about rising from the ashes. It made me think about my father. Why couldn't he have done what I am doing? He just gave up and ran."

"But didn't you give up in a way too?"

"I didn't leave my family behind!" Renee stated, emphatically.

"Not physically, but emotionally you did. There are many different ways of running and hiding, my dear. At least now you are running to something."

Renee agreed. Everything Erika said was true, even if it hurt to hear it at times. She felt like she was finally getting her life back again. It took taking a chance on hiring someone new for the universe to open up a whole slew of possibilities for her. She was ready for the journey.

They completed their session, and Erika wrote down Renee's next appointment time for three weeks away.

"So, where are you going on vacation?"

Erika started cleaning up the coffee area. "I am going to the south with my mother and sister. We're going to check out Georgia and the Carolinas. We have been planning this for a year."

"I have never taken a summer vacation. I never minded it, but sometimes I think about it."

Erika threw out some napkins that she used to clean up the counter. "Well, perhaps someday you will be able to. You never know."

"I don't see how. My business is seasonal."

Erika pointed to the ceiling. Renee raised her eyebrows.

"Possibilities, Renee. You never know what's right around you. Anything is possible if you really want something."

When Renee was walking out to her car, she pondered the last thoughts Erika shared with her. Then, it was as if the clouds opened up in the sky revealing an opening she never knew was there. It hadn't been there before, but now it was. Renee smiled. It wasn't the right time now, but perhaps next year. Like Erika said, there are possibilities.

Chapter 27

The fourth of July weekend was another successful one for Serenity Savor. Renee was really getting well-known in the town, especially due to her highly-reputed baked goods. She was working like crazy, but she loved every minute of it. Heather was receiving very high accolades at the Paddlewheel for how well she was handling the bar as Manager. She even came up with her own drink concoction. She wanted to get more events in the club, so she started researching and connecting with event planners. She was definitely a mover and a shaker.

Nikki and Kevin quickly bonded with Gia and Evan, which I was thrilled about. Evan somehow managed to pay for two more tickets to get Nikki and Kevin on the same dinner cruise as us. I wondered what was going on, but maybe Evan is just feeling so grateful things are right in his world with Gia. She has been texting me about twenty times a day again, so I know she is very happy with the way things are.

Aside from working at Serenity Savor, Derek taught me how to do basic face-painting, so he hired me to help out at random events throughout the season. It felt like I was back in the classroom again, so I was grateful he allowed me to do it.

On Sunday, July 3rd, we all met at the motel prior to the dinner cruise. I treated myself to a new dress for the occasion and I wore my patriotic jewelry. I said hello to my new neighbors, who were grilling in their backyard. They have had me over for barbeques a couple of times. My social life has greatly improved since the winter.

The five of us walked to the steamboat docks and waited in line to board. Evan looked just as handsome as ever, and Gia was dressed in a beautiful black and white sundress. Kevin and Nikki were wearing dressy-casual clothing. The sun was going to start setting. I love the sunsets in the mountains. As we started to board, I silently thanked God that I was blessed with such marvelous friends.

We were seated by one of the huge windows and enjoyed a spectacular view of Lake George. Evan seemed a little nervous, but I didn't really give it much thought. I was too caught up in the view and the beautiful boat atmosphere. Our waitress took our drink orders;I ordered a White Russian this time since this was a special occasion. I saw Evan go up to the band leader and speak with him for a few minutes. I figured he was requesting some songs for him and Gia to dance to.

The steamboat started its voyage, and we all helped ourselves to an absolutely scrumptious buffet. All five of us were sharing stories and having a blast. Kevin and Nikki shared about living by the Jersey Shore. I mentioned about the time my grandmother went to the boardwalk with my family on a vacation, and we went on this water ride called the Log Flume. My grandmother, unbeknownst to us, washed her shoes with a liquid soap earlier that day. Well, of course, we all got wet, and when we stepped off the ride, we heard squishy sounds and bubbles rising up around us. They were coming from my grandmother's shoes because the flume water mixed with the soap! My four friends were belly-laughing. I don't get to see my grandmother as often as I would like. I want to change that after the summer.

After our stomachs were full, the band began playing and people started heading towards the dance floor. Nikki was one of them. Gia and Evan followed suit. Kevin and I stayed behind, but I didn't mind. I was enjoying watching my friends have a joyous time. Half way through the dancing, Evan wandered over to the band, and the song came to an end. The bandleader handed the microphone to Evan. Gia looked over at me. I shrugged my shoulders.

"Ladies and gentleman," Evan began, "I apologize for interrupting your evening, but I believe you will understand in a few minutes."

Oh my god! Oh my god! No, it couldn't be! OH MY GOD! I thought, as I watched what was unfolding before me.

Evan walked over to Gia and put an arm around her. She looked totally perplexed. Suddenly it made sense why Evan wanted all of us here tonight. OH MY GOSH, he was going to PROPOSE!

Evan continued, "You see, about two years ago, I met the most amazing, beautiful, and compassionate woman in the world. She's funny too, and she has put up with me all of this time. I lost my way a bit and came very close to ruining the best thing that has ever happened to me."

By now, Gia was crying. So was I.

"It took a very wise and wonderful person in our lives to help knock sense into me, and I vowed and declared I would never take my gorgeous girlfriend for granted again."

Evan got down on one knee and removed a small box. The whole steamboat crowd focused on him and Gia. Gia looked as if she was about to pass out.

"Gianna Jacobs, will you do me the amazing and incredible honor of being my wife?"

Gia was so overcome with emotion she couldn't even speak. She did manage to nod her head. This was her dream for so long. She grabbed hold of Evan and cried tears of joy. So did Evan. I saw him keep mouthing "I love you so much. I am so sorry." The crew, band, and guests all clapped and cheered. Kevin, Nikki, and I ran up to them and crushed them in a hug. We all wound up falling on top of each other, laughing and crying at the same time. When we finally untangled ourselves and got back up, the band played a popular song by the group Atlantic Star. Gia and Evan were in the spotlight, as they should have been. At one point, Evan's eyes locked with mine, and I knew he was thanking me with his expression. I gave him a thumb's up. This was the start of a magnificent journey for my two best friends in the world.

Epilogue

I was standing on the sundeck watching the fireworks. They were exquisite tonight, lighting up the night sky with deep, bright shades of blue, purple, green, and gold. They would show the fireworks through Labor Day. As I took in each work of fire art, I couldn't help reflect on how my life has changed in less than a year. In some ways, I was like one of these firecrackers. I was this little cherry bomb just waiting to burst and reveal my true colors. Sometimes when it bursts, it isn't always pretty. Sometimes there are loud booms. In the end, the final product is a beautiful illumination, though.

When an unexpected event tears apart our lives, there is a shift in what we have always held true. Nothing is familiar. We cling desperately to anything that reminds us of the life we once knew, even if it was full of disappointment and disillusionment. Fear takes over, and we become paralyzed in our own bodies, even though we are still able to walk.

Last February I was offered an opportunity to work for Serenity Savor Motel. At first, I was hesitant to take it because it was nothing like what I had done before or went to school for. I could have said no, but I decided to go with the shift and see where it led. I now have a new career and purpose.

My boss Renee took a chance on a new desk clerk even though she had a negative experience the summer before and was in the red financially. She had every reason to say no, but instead she followed the shift, and her motel is starting to thrive again.

My friends Gia and Evan almost let circumstances and anxiety destroy the love that was so strong between them. They could have broken up and gone separate ways, but instead they chose to shift their priorities. Now they are planning the wedding of their dreams.

I haven't heard anything further from Kendra, but I know she cared enough to reach out even though she was going through chaos. I know I will hear from her again.

The finale of the fireworks is happening above me. Renee has already approached me about working next year at the motel. Keith offered me a job at the ski lodge for the winter. The sky is now dark. The fireworks have ended. My adventures, however, have only just begun. I can't wait to see what comes next.

Author's Note

I am thankful for the opportunity to bring Knight Shift into your lives. My hope and prayer is that it inspires you to look at the bigger picture when a shift occurs in your own life and how you may help empower someone else along the way.

I highly welcome engagement and feedback from my readers, I strongly encourage you to connect with me through my website www.suzannelaVoiewrites.com and follow me on YouTube, Facebook, and Instagram. Please continue to check the website for upcoming events. I look forward to hearing from you!

Please be on the lookout for the launch of Volume 2 set for spring of 2018! Sage Knight will be back for the next phase of her personal journey in the majestic setting of the Adirondack mountains.

Thank you all from the depths of my heart!

SL